Culturally Conscious Decision-Making for School Leaders
A Toolkit for Creating a More Equitable School Culture

Shauna McGee

Routledge
Taylor & Francis Group
NEW YORK AND LONDON

Designed cover image: © Getty Images

First published 2025
by Routledge
605 Third Avenue, New York, NY 10158

and by Routledge
4 Park Square, Milton Park, Abingdon, Oxon, OX14 4RN

Routledge is an imprint of the Taylor & Francis Group, an informa business

© 2025 Shauna McGee

The right of Shauna McGee to be identified as author of this work has been asserted in accordance with sections 77 and 78 of the Copyright, Designs and Patents Act 1988.

All rights reserved. The purchase of this copyright material confers the right on the purchasing institution to photocopy or download pages which bear the support material icon and a copyright line at the bottom of the page. No other parts of this book may be reprinted or reproduced or utilised in any form or by any electronic, mechanical, or other means, now known or hereafter invented, including photocopying and recording, or in any information storage or retrieval system, without permission in writing from the publishers.

Trademark notice: Product or corporate names may be trademarks or registered trademarks, and are used only for identification and explanation without intent to infringe.

ISBN: 978-1-032-76535-8 (hbk)
ISBN: 978-1-032-75870-1 (pbk)
ISBN: 978-1-003-47892-8 (ebk)

DOI: 10.4324/9781003478928

Typeset in Palatino
by SPi Technologies India Pvt Ltd (Straive)

Access the Support Material: www.routledge.com/9781032758701

Culturally Conscious Decision-Making for School Leaders

This exciting new book provides school leaders with a highly effective framework for culturally responsive and equity-driven leadership. School culture is how you lead, how your core values are represented in the work you do daily, and how stakeholders are impacted by what you choose. Author and educator Shauna McGee helps you grapple with the technical and adaptive challenges of developing an effective culture, and you'll learn how to shape your school culture by applying a culturally responsive lens to your decision-making. Each chapter in this practical book explores a different area of decision-making – including vision, budgeting, instructional programming, capacity building, and use of data. Full of rich examples, takeaway rubrics, and questions for self-reflection, this book is designed for current and aspiring school leaders who want to develop an equitable and student-centered culture.

Shauna McGee is Assistant Principal in the Bronx, NY. She is an English teacher and centers her leadership on culturally responsive curriculum and instructional practices in both learning and relationships.

Also Available from Routledge Eye On Education
(www.routledge.com/eyeoneducation)

Fostering Parent Engagement for Equitable and Successful Schools: A Leader's Guide to Supporting Families and Students

Teacher Leadership Practice in High-Performing Schools: A Blueprint for Excellence
Jeremy D. Visone

Finding Your Path as a Woman in School Leadership: A Guide for Educators, Allies, and Advocates
Kim Cofino and Christina Botbyl

Improving Teacher Morale and Motivation: Leadership Strategies that Build Student Success
Ronald Williamson and Barbara R. Blackburn

A Leadership Playbook for Addressing Rapid Change in Education: Empowered for Success
Teresa L. San Martín

Lead with Truth: How to Make a Difference in Your School, Your Life, and the Lives of Your Students
Qiana O'Leary

When Black Students Excel: How Schools Can Engage and Empower Black Students
Joseph F. Johnson, Jr., Cynthia L. Uline, and Stanley J. Munro, Jr.

Mismeasuring Schools' Vital Signs: How to Avoid Misunderstanding, Misinterpreting, and Distorting Data
Steve Rees and Jill Wynns

Leading School Culture through Teacher Voice and Agency
Sally J. Zepeda, Philip D. Lanoue, David R. Shafer, Grant M. Rivera

Contents

Preface vi
Meet the Author xiii
Online Supplemental Resources xiv

1 Introduction: Core Values and Self-Interrogation: Who. Are. You? 1

2 "For the [School] Culture" 18

3 School Culture and Shared Values: What's the V.I.B.E? 38

4 Budgeting: What ya Pockets Lookin' Like? 56

5 Instructional Core: You *Are* What They *Teach*! 76

6 Capacity Building: That's Your People? 99

7 Data and Progress Monitoring: Numbers Don't Lie, Right? 118

8 Sustainability and Your Legacy: Were You Official? 141

Additional Resources 151
Rubric for Culturally Conscious Decision-Making 153

Preface

"Do you want to impact 30 kids, or 300?" This was the question my principal asked me when I was laughing at the idea of being an assistant principal. I'm a stubborn one, and to this day, I refer to this question to ground me when I am having a hard time remembering why I signed up for this role. Leading in any capacity is challenging work, but being a school leader is next level. You are an adult wrangler, the parent whisperer, the being who knows all things without actually knowing most things, and you have to do this all with a smile and keeping your mental health in order. Oh wait, did I mention those test scores and that data better be on point, too?! I share my sentiment to be transparent about the fact that I did not see myself as an administrator and struggle still to feel like I made the right choice. I love teaching, could have retired a teacher, and still seek out opportunities to teach almost daily.

Leadership means being the person who ultimately is responsible for all decisions made or not made. In a school building, there are so many decisions to make it can be overwhelming, especially if you are someone like me who is consumed with how the decisions impact everyone involved. There is no decision in a school community that does not reverberate across teams and groups, and owing to this, leaders need to be reflective about how they choose to make these decisions. I did not see myself as a leader, because although I was a strong teacher, I dealt with, and still deal with, imposter syndrome. I knew I taught my heels off, so why did I not see myself as capable of leading alongside adults? This was due to my anxiety of how these decisions would impact my perception in the community. Choose to do something that negatively impacted teachers but benefitted students? Did this mean I would now lose teacher support? Forgot to send that email about the parent engagement event and as a result no one showed up? Would that mean people would think

I intentionally did so? All of these questions were valid but also don't matter.

This book came to be because I went from Master Teacher to reluctant administrator through the direction of my dope mentor, who is my current principal. Through our daily engagement, discussions, and his willingness to be a model for culturally conscious leadership practices daily, I am able to see that the real driving force behind all of my outcomes and desires as a leader is rooted in the decisions that were once the bane of my existence. Making decisions is not the only predictor of your success as a school leader as all they require is a decisive nature. **How you make the decisions will be the deciding factor for your success as a school leader.** The how is predicated on the who, and sometimes we are not always reflective about who we are and where we can challenge or push our belief systems. This is true of moments in my own leadership. I believe that school culture is the most important and primary factor a school leader cultivates or disrupts to achieve all other ends. This is done through the decisions they make in various spaces daily and should be driven by their "Head and Heart".

The "How"

Overall, this book is about providing you with a deep understanding of how to lead a school community and Imbue the culture you desire through the decisions you make on a daily basis. While the discourse around school culture is often oriented with its being a subset of leadership, I believe that it is the most important element and that we as leaders create culture based on how we move daily. In the case of this book, the way you move as a leader is driven by your leadership decisions and their impacts on the community. This is written for anyone who is a school leader—principal, assistant/vice principal, or leadership team member—or anyone else who is part of making decisions that will reverberate across the community. This definitely includes department leaders and coaches. I would also argue that all members of a school community should get into this text as it offers insight into how a community is impacted by the challenges "behind the curtain". This book is also for folks in leadership programs who want to become school leaders and would like a lens on what it takes to lead a school community in a way that is culturally conscious. The difference between being *culturally responsive* and *culturally conscious* is that a culturally responsive leader is responding to the needs of the community (community-facing; outward) based on information obtained whereas a culturally conscious leader is also driven by the constant reflection on their own belief systems and interactions with others as the driving force for their interaction with the community (reflection-based; inward).

We're all busy, and if reading cover to cover isn't your jam, I get it. This book was written with the intent of your being able to read the chapters in alignment with what speaks to your current need, and each chapter has a specific component of leadership impacted by decision-making. In layman's terms, read this out of order if your ancestors tell you to! The chapters are independent of one another, and your understanding will not be impacted. Now let's get this work! Here is a snapshot of each:

Chapter 1 is the introduction and focuses on setting the foundation for who you are and how you show up as a leader. By focusing on your lived experiences and "core values," this chapter orients the focus on your belief systems as a person and as a school leader.

Chapter 2 provides a formula for determining the "V.I.B.E" of your community and assessing what it possesses as a lever for establishing what elements are missing. The purpose of this is to be asset-minded before attempting to develop a culture reflective of what you desire.

Chapter 3 taps into the all-elusive budgeting component and asks, "What ya pockets lookin' like," aligned with decision-making. In this chapter, you will reflect on what it means to make culturally conscious decisions even in the face of adversity and budgetary constraints.

Chapter 4, my personal favorite, asks you what you desire as a leader when it comes to the instructional core aligned with curriculum and instruction. While you are no longer a teacher, you are still an educator and must center what's best for young people who will be active participants in society. This chapter also introduces the V.I.B.E model for curriculum and instruction and provides a strategy for interrogating a curriculum for culturally responsive elements.

Chapter 5 helps you determine how to ensure that you are spreading the wealth and investing in leaders within your community. Ever feel overwhelmed or anticipate not having the expertise necessary for a particular role? Then this chapter on capacity building is for you!

Chapter 6 dives into data and monitoring progress. One of the most important measures of a school is how people talk about what you've done. This chapter will address the formal measures that leaders need to consider but will also address the secondary, invisible metrics that should also be evaluated when determining the effectiveness of an initiative, program, or team. This chapter also addresses grading and how to use data as a measure for improving in all areas, not just objective, finite measures.

Last but certainly not least, the summative *Chapter 7* focuses on how to reflect on your leadership. Were you an effective leader who planned for all possibilities and eventualities? Or did you allow your hubris to thrive at the forefront of your leadership? Did you plan for a successor or will your community have to endure another culture shift if there is a new leader? This chapter will aid you in understanding how to center yourself, be real about your growth areas, and reflect on all you have or have not done—all aimed at leaving the community in a better place than where you found it.

Having trouble with budgeting? Chapter 3 is for you. Want to deepen your lens on being a culturally responsive instructional leader? Read Chapter 4. I would ask, though, that you read Chapter 1. Our core values and leadership mindset are clues into how we will impact a community as leaders. The work in that chapter is foundational and will ask you to see who you are not just as a leader but as a human being and educator overall. Inclusive of our roles are our race, lived experiences, and belief systems about children and families. Without this work we are remiss in the opportunity placed before us to shape lives as leaders.

Because I want this work to be transferable, there are some special features. At the end of each chapter there is a rubric specific to that chapter's focus. Example, for the "Budgeting" chapter there is a rubric at the end that provides a scale to determine your level of cultural consciousness aligned to budgetary decision-making. The same is true of every chapter and its focus area. You will also find suggested reads at the end of each chapter that expand on the topics and add an additional layer of learning. At the end of the book you will find "additional materials". These are supplemental reads not included in the chapters as well as the completed rubric encompassing all chapters. The aim of this rubric is for you to use it as a guide. All decisions have the power to inform a school's culture and as a result, the rubric should be used to be proactive as well as reflect and plan. Each chapter also contains modeled examples, exercises to think through and a rubric for assessment on how to cultivate a VIBE for your community. "For the [School] Culture" was the original title of this book and you will see it often. This should be a mantra that drives your decisions as we ultimately desire to create a school culture that reflects what our communities need inclusive of all subgroups and demographics.

The "Vibes"

Before you get into big boss tings' there are some understandings we need to unpack together. This book is written in my authentic voice. As a Black woman who is a professional student and has read a copious amount of literature on leadership and education, it was important for me to speak in a manner that was free of dense, jargon laden terms. I wanted the learning to be accessible and also personable. Having taught for over 10 years so many of my students found themselves struggling to write because they did not feel like they had access to academic language. Imagine the power associated with knowing that all language is language, and that it is not a signifier of being less than. Language can be used to exclude and if I'm being honest, speaking in my authentic voice is liberating. Yes, I use academic terms that are leadership-oriented blah blah, but I also include terms that are familiar to those closest to me. Here are some definitions for terms you may be unfamiliar with but are an integral part of helping form our understanding as we work through the chapters:

- **Assessment**: Objectively auditing for the purposes of determining elements present and/or lacking
- **Haters**: Dissenters or anyone who is problem-naming but not solution-suggesting or willing to work toward a solution
- **The "Streets"**: Synonyms: stakeholder, community member. Anyone who is part of the school community and contributes to its functioning; individuals who can be used to elicit formal and informal feedback (i.e., people who are never explicitly named but "I heard" this from them)
- **"Opp"**: Opposition or anyone who stands to disrupt a mission or goal; can be intentional or unintentional
- **"Vibe"**: A feeling or energy that permeates a space and can be felt or omitted by others
- **"Head, Heart, Hands"**: This is a model provided for decision-making that includes a leader's thought process (*Head*), core values (*Heart*), and potential impacts of decision (Hands) on a community
- **V.I.B.E [School Culture Edition]**: Acronym for assessing school culture by using feedback and data from the *V*oice of the community, *I*nquiry, *B*lessings, and *E*nvironment (Chapter 2)
- **V.I.B.E [Curriculum and Instruction Edition]**: Acronym for assessing curriculum and instruction by auditing for *V*aried *V*oices, *I*nquisition opportunities, *B*ackwards Design, and *E*xtensions (Chapter 4)

Being a school leader should be a vibe! You should be able to reflect on your "Head and Heart" aligned with culturally conscious decision-making and show up in your community in a way that ensures that all marginalized groups are considered in your leadership. If you are reading this and have any doubt about your ability to lead teams or a school, you are starting in the right place. Doubt is the manifestation of caring so much about the outcome that you tell yourself you can't do it before you try. On the other hand, if you are reading this and are in a space of hubris—that is, "What can this book tell me about running a community?"—I still implore you to read as I can guarantee you will find many things to address your day-to-day responsibilities that are not laid out for you in those expensive leadership preparation programs. I cannot guarantee reading this will shift your heart, but I can promise this book will make you think about your leadership differently and inform you of what work needs to be done for when you are ready. Being a school leader, you should always do it "For the [School] culture," and I'm blessed you are allowing me to VIBE with you!

Meet the Author

Shauna McGee, M.A., M.S.Ed., Ed.M., is a dope educator and professional student hailing from Queens, whose career has been dedicated to teaching English in the Bronx. Notable for her expertise, she has excelled as a Master Teacher and served as an exemplary Teacher Leader, utilizing culturally responsive practices. Her unwavering commitment to educational excellence has been instrumental in supporting schools throughout New York City. Shauna's leadership philosophy is deeply rooted in the development of culturally responsive curricula and instructional methodologies, emphasizing the importance of inclusive learning environments and fostering meaningful relationships with students and families. Currently, she holds the position of assistant principal, where her visionary approach to curriculum and instruction continues to inspire and elevate the educational experience for young people and those who nurture them. Shauna will be publishing another book on culturally responsive curriculum adoption and adaptation, called *You Are What You Teach*, with Routledge press. She is also a wife and mommy to two nuggets, Sebastian and Sydney.

Online Supplemental Resources

Some of the resources in this book can be accessed online by visiting this book's product page on our website: www.routledge.com/9781032758701 (then follow the links indicating support material, which you can then download directly).

- Additional Reads to Promote Equity and Shape your Head, Heart, and Hands
- Rubric for Culturally Conscious Decision-Making

1

Introduction

Core Values and Self-Interrogation: Who. Are. You?

You've decided to become a school leader. You're either a masochist looking for a daily dose of chaos, you were/are a strong teacher and believe you can lead others, or you are doing it to "make a difference for the kids". All of these responses require an obligatory eye roll as the job you signed up for is thankless and requires you to have a deep understanding of your growth areas while also be willing to accept unsolicited feedback that will almost always put you in your feelings. These "feelings" can range from self-doubt to inadequacy. You also need an understanding that your role is that of manager rather than the head honcho who gets to make all the decisions. Do you love teaching and learning and think becoming an administrator will allow you to deepen your impact or influence these areas? You are signing up for the wrong role. Are you someone who wants to lead others because you pride yourself on having "natural leadership abilities" (i.e., have been lauded for your ability to be brash and tell others what to do)? You are also in the wrong role and are in for a rude awakening. You will have the opportunity to shape and influence the minds of others, but the "how" will look very different than you anticipate. Sure, you will be a leader in title, but the skills you need for this to be successful were not taught in that expensive leadership program.

While this introduction seems cynical, it is important to understand that school leadership requires a special set of skills not everyone possesses. Later, we will discuss the different roles of classroom teacher, instructional coach, and administrator, but we must set the foundation of this chapter with the understanding that being a leader in general takes work that is not all "technical" (Heifetz, 1994). Being a *school leader* requires introspection, constant self-assessment, willingness to trust and support others, and the ability to pivot at a moment's notice. Rigidity, hubris, and taking things to the chest are all attributes which will lead to your ultimate departure from the profession. These attributes can also lead to a lack of results for the young people you serve, because those you serve don't respect or value your leadership. Still want to be a school leader? Good for you. If not, still keep reading and laugh at what other optimists such as myself signed up for.

Part 1: Personal, Local, and Immediate Experiences: Core Values

Becoming an educator made me hyper-aware of the way race impacts people's perceptions of you. Growing up in Queens and then living in Brooklyn, I did not have too many instances where I felt I did not belong. While there were moments of turbulence in my elementary and high school experience, I did not have to think of my race or address it much in my adolescent life. I was loved and affirmed daily at home. When I began teaching, I was fortunate to carry these positive experiences over into my career as the community was diverse—inclusive of staff and students. Then my first parent–teacher conference came and I was hype! I had two master's degrees, was 24 years old in a career that brought me joy, and was obsessed with literacy and seeing my kids win. You couldn't tell me nothin'! I just knew my lens on reading and writing would shake up a classroom as I desired to be the teacher I did not have. One parent walked into my classroom with her daughter, and the look on her face told me she was confused. I introduced myself and said "hey" to the student who was happy to see me. As we walked to sit down and talk, the parent did not say a word. To break the ice, I started by asking if she had any questions or concerns before I went into my spiel and she said, "You're her ELA [English language arts] teacher?" I said "yeah, I look young, but I promise I'm legal to teach"— thinking my age was the reason for the inquiry, I attempted to make a light-hearted joke. The mom continued, "Where did you go to school? Are you from here?" Of course, excitedly I rattled off my degrees and where I graduated from to calm her. The meeting continued and went well in my opinion. Her daughter was bright, sweet, and was one of my biggest helpers. I did not think much of this interaction, but as the years continued, I was asked on more than one occasion "where I went to school" and when I rattled them off each time, there was a sense of relief from the inquisitor. As I talked to colleagues about parent–teacher conferences, others informed me that these questions were not a regular inquiry during their conferences. Was it me? Did I give off scatterbrain and this is why the inquiries persisted? Even as an assistant principal, I have had parents in shock that *I* am the assistant principal. While the questions are more coded, they all allude to the same question—are you qualified to educate? As I am now 10+ years removed from my first conference, these occurrences always make me first think about the mental models that led to these questions. What does an ELA teacher look like? What does an assistant principal look like? If I don't meet the mold for this, who does, and why? The answers to these questions will vary because mental models are driven by what we are exposed to in our daily lives. This process is called "socialization". Sensoy and DiAngelo refer to socialization as "the process of learning the meaning and practices that enable us to make sense of and behave appropriately in [that] culture" (Sensoy and DiAngelo, 2017: 36). We make meaning of others through subscribing to the ideals of the culture we personally subscribe to *or* we act in response to the cultures of others based on our assumptions about their culture. As much as I want to discredit it because it makes me feel defeated, your race will play a role in your leadership whether you want it to or not. However, it is up to you to reflect on your experiences and project the version of yourself you want to be experienced. In my leadership, I find being my authentic self, leading with my core values at the forefront, and not shying away from difficult conversations work best. Some will read my example and say "well, who said it was race that drove the parent inquiries? Maybe they just wanted to know where you graduated from?" To those people, I'd describe what I was asked as "qualifying questions". These questions are inquiry-based but are driven by one's unspoken belief that the person under question needs to prove or justify their positioning aligned to the inquiry. Simply stated, you have a mental model that says a person does not meet what you believe to be attributes ascribed to the position or individual. It is my belief that I did not fit the model of what a teacher should look like based on race and, for that reason, I was asked qualifying questions. Let's entertain the idea of its not being race and say it was my womanhood that provoked the inquiry. That's still wack. Needing someone to provide information that aligns with your mental model of what is acceptable means there is some work that needs to be done regarding your belief system and what you were taught about certain groups of people. If you are more focused on the example and not my experience, I'd ask you to reflect. Are you someone who asks "qualifying" questions? To whom? What groups of people? What does that suggest about your beliefs around that particular group or position?

In his book *Courageous Conversations about Race*,[1] Glenn Singleton provides a framework for how to discuss topics and issues related to race. While this chapter does not discuss race as the driving factor for our core values, our identities and lived experiences are what drive our decisions, and inclusive of this is race. My leadership is driven by what I, as a Black woman who attended both public and private schools all her life, experienced in these spaces. This experience would vary for others based on race, ethnicity, familial income levels, and other factors. I would argue, though, that when we walk into a school on the first day as the new principal or administrator, our race is on full display and leads to unintentionally derived mental models about our leadership. Singleton's "Four Agreements" and "6 Conditions" provide a pathway for how to reflect on our own experiences and discuss issues of racial identity with others in a way that is productive and inquiry-based. Discussing race and how it has shaped who we are, and thus our decisions, requires tact, delicacy, and patience. This aspect of ourselves is one we cannot shy away from as leaders. Who you are should always include how your identity shows up in your leadership values and what you desire for your community. It is also important to speak transparently to these as well as the driving force for your personal value system. While you don't walk into a community and impart your value system, what you deem important will be reflected in the decisions you make.

Get to Know YOU!

One of the exercises in my leadership program was determining what my "core values" were—not as a leader but as a human being. Did I value equity, empathy, kindness, friendship, humility, liberation, bravery, and so on? Who knows! When asked to narrow down my own values, a task that should have been fairly simple, I struggled to choose three that spoke to me. First, I was worried about how my words would impact my peers' perception of me. But more importantly, I wanted to be connected to these words through my experiences. If I said I valued "liberation," could I speak to an example where I needed to be liberated or experienced liberating others? If I said "empathy," is this something I model as a teacher leader or administrator? Determining my core values helped me understand where my areas of growth were as I could easily identify with some based on my experiences but not others. My core values were "identity, honesty, and transparency". The areas I needed to work on? "Empathy, patience, and kindness". I was able to see that my core values lived in the way I planned lessons, coached, and how I gave feedback to others. However, I needed to be more kind in my approach to adults, practice more empathy, and understand that not everyone will produce the same outcomes as development takes time. When thinking about your core values, do so from the lens of your lived experiences and values you can personally speak to, not what you think a "model school" should be. It is very easy to have a dope school acronym that looks good on banners, but if you can't speak to how each of the letters in your school's mantra lives in your leadership, it is nothing more than a cool reminder of a vision without execution. It is also important to reflect on the values you do not connect with or embody, as these will be the values that define your leadership style and how you engage with the community. As an example, if you are someone who struggles with valuing "community," where does this come from? Have you ever been part of a community that made you feel safe? If you have not, what would it look like to create that for someone else?

Does a Fish Know It's Wet?!

We are all shaped by our lived experiences, and when we show up to work, these experiences, as well as what we've learned from them, show up with us. When I was a teacher, I saw myself in a high school in Brooklyn teaching a modern-day version of Shakespeare to 10th-grade Advanced Placement students. Needless to say, when I was hired to teach in the Bronx at a middle school after being ghosted by a Brooklyn high school, I was devastated to say the least. What I did not expect was all of the feelings that came with being told I would be starting my career in the Bronx. I had a pleasurable experience interviewing with the principal, he and the assistant principal came to see me teach, and I was offered the job right away! I had nothing but wonderful things to say about the process. Immediately, what went through my head was how awful the Bronx was, how terrible the kids would be, and how Doug Lemov's "Teach Like a Champion" techniques would be my go-to for "these kids"—something I later realized was not the model for how to build positive relationships with children of color or young people in general. Outside of the famous Bronx Zoo, I'd never been to the Bronx despite living in New York City my whole life. So where did these negative mental models come from? Of course, within one day of meeting them, students proved my negative mental models completely wrong and forced me to challenge my own biases and social conditioning. All of my mental models were impacted by what I saw on television and heard from others. The Bronx is continually represented as a place that is crime-ridden and appears lawless. The beauty of the Bronx and its residents, as well as the vibrant life here, are rarely shown. It is up to us as human beings to "unpack" our own bags of bias to discover the ugly truths about ourselves and our belief systems. We have to challenge what we choose to ingest. If the conditioning was so pervasive for me, it is and can be for everyone. When I was checked by a friend for being biased, I justified my irrational belief system about this community and doubled-down on my conclusions. "Let's keep it a buck, the Bronx is never on the news for anything positive," "those kids are always shooting up the street," "name one good thing that came out of the Bronx?!" It wasn't until I received more pushback from another friend, an intervention if you will, that I really looked inward and had to evaluate my own mental models and value system. Did I believe in transparency, honesty, and identity for all kids? Or just those who lived in certain communities? Would I want someone to look at me or my neighborhood and decide I wasn't worthy or capable? I'm married to a Black man whom I was then dating. He lived in the Bronx and partly grew up there. What did that suggest about my mental models of him? Phew. The unpacking I had to do was ugly and uncomfortable. I was fortunate to have people around me who cared enough to tell me the truth and not care how I received it. It also required a willingness to listen in my own time. Luckily for me, I quickly realized my ignorance and pushed up against it with real examples of excellence and dope energies—this came in the form of my first-ever 7th-grade class. This negative thinking was ubiquitous, and if I had allowed it to thrive unchecked, it would have undoubtedly extended to my belief systems about families. Imagine if I had gone forward in my career believing that children from the Bronx were all dangerous. This would have shown up in how I treated them, educated them, and even perceived their ability. This was such a low point for me as a Black woman. To inherently devalue a group of people on the basis of the perception of others and media is never okay. I was just so unaware. I am a firm believer that you begin to believe what you say and think. Once we have a mental model of something or someone, all we see are examples of things that affirm our position. This is why we need systems, structures, and people to disrupt our thinking as much as possible.

I speak on my own need to self-reflect about my social conditioning to connect to how we as educators show up in all of our spaces. School leaders don't always have honest and objective avenues for honest critiques and feedback. How many of us are willing to tell our bosses they're bugging? As a teacher, we teach what we have to but also teach what we value. When I had the chance to choose the novel for my class, I chose *Native Son* by Richard Wright because I saw Bigger Thomas[2] in my community every day—the novel spoke to me. For those who have not had experiences in urban communities and consume their knowledge of these spaces only through the lens of media or narratives of others, of course, the perception will be skewed. We also listen to and receive anecdotal notes from people whose opinions we value. If my grandmother says the Bronx is dangerous and filled with crime, it MUST be so. I love her, she's kind, and she would never steer me wrong, right? We cannot avoid socialization, so how do we go about forming and challenging our opinions? There are questions below to help you determine what you believe and why you believe it. This serves as a self-assessment and reflection before you begin to include others in your self-reflection process.

TABLE 1.1 5 Why's of Self-Reflection

1. *What* do you believe about (insert group, race, ideology, topic, etc.)?
2. *When* was your earliest memory of when you experienced or learned about this?
3. *Who* or *What* is driving your belief system?
    a. What are you consuming aligned to this? Readings, news stations, personal experience, experiences of others?
    b. Are they all of the same viewpoint?
4. *Where* does this fall in alignment to your core values?
    a. What do you believe to be true? Do you seek out, or are you willing to find, alternate narratives?
5. *Why* do you believe what you do? Is this belief harmful or biased against certain groups?

After you reflect on these questions, it is important to talk to others and determine what others believe your values are. Specifically, do others know what your belief systems and opinions about particular topics or groups?. This inquiry will allow for layered reflection and will help you determine if what you believe is exuded in your interactions with others. Start with your closest friends and family members to obtain a picture of who you are as a person through the eyes of those who love you most. Your family and friends in most cases choose to be part of your world, but they are also often the ones who are least critical because they love you! Also, these are the people we tend to be the least kind to, as we know they love us, and other than a disagreement, there is no pressure or indictment attached to our loved ones' view of us. Asking what they believe about you based on their interactions and experiences with you can prove powerful. If your core values are kindness, grace, and patience, do you exude these in your interactions with your family? When I took my teacher leader survey results to my family—that I was sometimes intense and scary, sometimes off-putting, and a perfectionist whose expectations were too high—I just knew they would disagree and feel like the people who gave the feedback were crazy! I was wrong. So wrong. So what did I do? Of course, I became upset and defensive. I immediately asked why no one told me! The response was "we knew you'd do what you're doing right now…you ask for feedback and then explain why we're wrong". They were 100% correct. I share this to explain feedback from others, especially those closest to you can be telling, but you have to be willing to receive it and sit with it. The expectation is not to change overnight but to be cognizant and aware of how you show up in all spaces. Next step is including another layer of voice. Self-interrogation through community feedback has entered the chat.

Part 2: Self-Interrogation Through Community Feedback

Self-interrogation sounds simple enough, but doing it correctly requires a level of humility that has to be trained and sustained. We're all human and critiques often hurt or feel like an attack—especially if they were not solicited. For our purposes, self-interrogation is defined as a person's ability to challenge and question what they believe through intentionally seeking *critical* feedback. When we are lauded for the things we do well, it is easy to be reflective. Example: "Chantel loved the way I led that meeting, she told me when I asked her". In this example, many things can be true at once. One, Chantel might have enjoyed the meeting because she was on TikTok looking at end-of-year teacher posts. Two, Chantel might have loved the meeting because she shares and values your type-A leadership style. Three, everyone except Chantel hated it because you ask for feedback but then qualify what feedback you disagree with by providing asterisks for *why*. No one asked for that. It is also important to understand your positionality as the leader will impact the authenticity and truthfulness of the feedback you receive. Some will tell you the truth because it's who they are, and others out of fear, disdain, apathy, or lack of interest will not say anything at all. The silent feedback is the one we need most as it will push us to think deeply and become reflective about what led to that feedback. Dissenters have the best suggestions! But we'll talk more about this in Chapter 6. In my example of my narrative about the Bronx, my friend was willing to push back against my insanity because of our pre-established relationship. I also hope she pushed back because my actions over the years did not align with what I was communicating. If I were her boss, the feedback might not have come at all. To truly be ready to receive critical feedback, though, we need to follow a formula!

    Before we start applying a formula, we have to come to an understanding about a few things. The *"streets"* encompasses anyone in your community you are able to elicit feedback from both by request and what gets back to you from people engaging casually in discourse with one another. This applies to both personal and professional relationships. The streets are not ever going to reveal who specifically said what but will provide the information via various sources. For example, a staff member comes to you and says, "I heard you are planning to move people to different grades." To this information, you have to understand the following:

1. You can never ask who said what. The streets don't tell. You will get a generalized statement provided to you—for example, I heard you were planning to hire another gym teacher—and you have to just roll with it no matter how untrue or silly.
2. Unpack the statement through inquiry and not defensiveness. Always give the streets information to take back. You control the narrative only if you participate in the discussion. Does that mean you let your right hand know what your left is doing? No. It simply means all information is valuable and you are able to respond with the level of engagement you believe to be appropriate. This doesn't mean giving out false information either. It means engaging in discourse based on the information you've obtained without sharing anything the streets are not privy to. For the example above about the grade changes, you have to realize the person saying it might just be speaking from a place of anxiety and nothing has been said about moving anyone. The other possibility is the streets did say that. You can respond in one of two ways. You can completely shut down the rumor and say "nope. We're keeping things the way they are for now". You can leave the door open and affirm that there may be some change but assure them that everything will be transparent and include staff voice. You can—if this comment is something you have no desire to engage with—use my personal favorite phrase "that's crazy". This tells the person there is no fishing for information but may also unintentionally affirm their suspicions. The response you provide will be based on the message you want to communicate, or not.

TABLE 1.2 The Formula: How to find out what the *STREETS* say about you?

1. Ask for *critical* feedback about your leadership and engagement *specifically*.
2. Once you receive the feedback, speak to what trends you notice.
3. Get out of your feelings!

LAST STEP: Reflect on what you want to change; ACT on it over time, not immediately.

Now for the work! Diving into each of these areas briefly, it is important to start with how you ask for feedback. You should communicate to staff you will ask for feedback but want to do so anonymously. This lets people know you value their opinions and are looking to do better. The hiccup for most people is having to submit the feedback to the person who does the evaluations. No bueno. Provide the questions to a colleague, trusted teacher, or someone else in the community to distribute. This will ensure you are far removed from those taking the survey and are only the recipient of the data which comes from it. Once you receive the feedback, internalize it and understand that you may not have the opportunity to ask more questions or consolidate what you've learned. Internalization looks like taking the data in all its good and bad parts and asking yourself about the "why" as well as possible contributing factors. This is difficult for me as I want to immediately control the narrative. Too bad.

Of course, you will want to know who said "you can do better with being more present", even though you were in the hallway for 30 minutes the day you gave the survey! You can't know who said what as this will certainly impact your perception of the data. Who said what also doesn't really matter as perception becomes reality for most. Focusing on the 'who' instead of the 'what' will certainly taint the message even if it is something you need to hear. What's important is what the streets are saying about you. You want to know if there are large trends that need to be addressed or if there are particular groups who view you differently. Does your school office staff view you as more polite and warm than your teachers? Do students know who you are? Are you a presence for non-school staff? As much as you want to, do not immediately move into action to change things. We naturally default to wanting to fix things that are viewed as deficits, but there are many reasons for our areas of growth. Moving immediately to 'fix things' sends the message you did not internalize the data and are exclusively worried about your perception. True change and self-interrogation take time. Use the data as a starting point to have deeper conversations, take an inquiry stance, and learn WHY the behaviors or attributes are manifesting in your leadership. Most importantly, determine if how you're perceived aligns with your core values. Have you ever been wronged and had someone immediately tell you all of the changes they'd make to improve things? How'd that work out? While you haven't wronged anyone directly, it can feel that way to the community based on decisions you've made or how you present in different spaces. When we offer immediate promises, the outcome is almost never what was intended and that is because changing fundamental parts of who we are or deeply learning about ourselves is not an overnight process. More so than changing, learning about how who you are impacts others is transformative. Don't make promises you may not follow through without asking yourself very important questions. In the "Core Values" section at the end, there are model questions you can use to reflect, interrogate and challenge how you present and are perceived by others. Most importantly, get out of your feelings and understand how the information makes you feel before you talk over trends and feedback you've received. It is integral to talk over the feedback with your community so they understand that you value their voice and desire to use it. You can also speak to trends you don't believe align with who you are or who you desire to be. This shows you are thoroughly reflecting on how you show up for others. Remind yourself that self-interrogation is for the greater good of the community. Endearing trust, having people feel valued, and contributing to the community by using their voice is the ultimate goal. Remember, you catch more bees with honey than vinegar. Feedback will always show dissenting opinions. There will always be challengers or dissent to your leadership model because you can't be everything to everyone at once. This is okay and par for the course as a leader. Take the feedback as it can't all be good. If you're anything like me, you should be your own worst critic anyway. No one can say anything to me I haven't already said to myself. Now that I say that out loud, that's not healthy… is it?

For those who will ask, "Where's the culturally responsive leadership here? It's just taking feedback from staff!?" Intentionally seeking *critical* feedback about your leadership and how you model what you believe to be your values are both elements of being culturally responsive. These things require you to understand how your own culture and socialization impact the energy and mental models you bring into a community. True self-interrogation also requires you to have an understanding of the interactions of your own culture and lived experiences with those of other races, ethnicities, abilities, genders, economic status, and more. Your beliefs drive your decisions and these decisions impact the actions of others when you are a leader. Know who you are, what you believe, and push up against it with every bone in your body if there are elements of your belief systems that need to be questioned. Also use this knowledge to be reflective, open to feedback, and check your ego at the door. This will ensure you are in a perpetual stage of improvement. It is not easy, but it is what's best to keep you centered in what's best for the community as opposed to satisfying your hubris. The rubric below provides a succinct self-assessment opportunity as you navigate self-interrogation. The rubric begins at the "entering" stage and progresses to "deepening". Growth and learning are not linear and this process will be fluid. Just as no teacher "lives" in the highly effective area every day of their career, it is important that you as a leader understand that, as your community shifts, so will your level of willingness and approach to self-interrogation. Nothing fun is easy! Once you arrive at deepening, continue to push yourself and continually reflect on what areas or aspects of yourself can be deepened or challenged. The piece of feedback I received as a coach about my affect that puts me in my feelings? That I'm "aloof," meaning kind but cold. Very accurate, but they didn't have to read me like that.

Core Values and Self-Interrogation: Who. Are. You?
Application and Materials

Core Values and Self-Interrogation Who. Are. You?

Entering	Emerging	Applying	Deepening
I understand the importance of feedback and receive it from my colleagues. I can acknowledge that my lived experience impacts my leadership and core values.	I understand the importance of feedback and receive/welcome it from everyone regardless of level and use it to reflect on my decisions and leadership. I can acknowledge that my race, ethnicity, and lived experiences impact my leadership and core values.	I seek/solicit critical feedback from the school community and reflect on how my perceptions or beliefs impact the decisions I make as a leader. I am intentional about exploring how my lived experiences may have created unconscious bias in my leadership/core values.	I seek/solicit feedback from all stakeholders and am also intentional about deepening my knowledge to disrupt negative narratives through literature, immersion, or "courageous conversations". I am aware of some of my unconscious bias, and I work to undo them and reflect on where these may show up in my leadership/core values.

Activity

Core Value Leadership Activity

Answer the following questions to determine what your core values are as a PERSON before examining what you'd like them to be for your school community. Your values are driven by your identity and experiences. After you answer all of these, begin to craft your leadership values.

Core Value Leadership Activity

Part 1: Inquiry and Investigation

1. What is your RACIAL identity? How has this impacted you as a child? As an adult? As a professional?
2. How has your identity (race, orientation, education, income/familial income) impacted your educational experiences?
3. Assess the demographics of your school community. What narratives were you told about them, or what are the belief systems you have about these groups?
4. What experiences do you want your students, staff, and family to have at your school community?

Part 2: Core Values

1. Select 10 values you believe are important to you based on the questions above.
2. Narrow them down to five.
3. Write a short narrative explaining why those values matter to you as a leader and what you hope to achieve with implementing them.
   a. This will help when you have to explain why you selected your core values as a leader and can serve as a driving force for whole-school values.

Scenario-Based Practice:

Take it to the streets: Scenario-Based Preparation

You've just accepted a job as a principal in a school community with staff that has a much different makeup than your racial identity. You've spent the first two months of the school year surveying and listening to staff about how the school can improve. Overall, it seems staff like things the way they are, but surveys show students want better relationships with their teachers and teachers need better relationships with one another.

How do you go about speaking to the data and sharing your personal core values? How do you create and establish buy-in with a staff whose racial make-up may present challenges for you, especially as a NEW principal?

<u>*Note*</u>: While racial disparity is not a predictor of dissent, it is one of the factors that can present a challenge for any person in a leadership role. Other challenges can be years of experience, age, gender, and so on. The car you drive can even cause there to be a negative perception. If you're focused on "race" being the factor in this scenario, we've got some work to do, and that's okay!

What are you consuming?
We Reading Over Here!

Notes

1 See Singleton (2015) for an in-depth overview of the protocol.
2 You have never read *Native Son* by Richard Wright? You have not LIVED!

References

Heifetz, R. A. (1994). *Leadership without easy answers*. Belknap Press of Harvard University Press.

Sensoy, Ö., & DiAngelo, R. J. (2017). *Is everyone really equal?: An introduction to key concepts in social justice education* (2nd ed.). Teachers College Press.

Singleton, G. E. (2015). *Courageous conversations about race: A field guide for achieving equity in schools*. Corwin, A Sage Company.

2

"For the [School] Culture"

"For the [School] Culture"

"Culture" is defined as characteristics of everyday life of a group of people located in a given time and place (Ozlem et al. 36). "For the Culture" is a colloquial term used most often by Black folks to signal their participation in an activity that aligns with their culture, Black culture to be specific. When a Black person says they are doing it "for the culture," they are performing their act as a representation of or affirmation of their culture and unspoken norms within it. For example, if using "slang" in an academic setting or a setting that is considered professional, one might say they are doing it "for the culture." While this seems like a minute occurrence, this can be an act of liberation. Without going too far off into a linguistics lesson, African-American Vernacular English (AAVE), Black English (BE), and Ebonics—for those who are unfamiliar with the academic terms—are often seen as inferior linguistic systems despite having legitimate rules and meeting the criteria for a well-defined language (Smitherman, 1996). While Black folks are often villainized or seen as unprofessional for utilizing AAVE, people of other races are seen as trendy or hip as they are deemed to be "tapped in" to what is popular (Alim and Smitherman, 2012). Doing it "for the culture" means taking a step toward what makes one feel whole and accepted and speaks to their heart. The takeaway here is that culture is ingrained within each person and their experiences. Culture can be shared, it can be adopted, but participation in it requires one to subscribe to its ideals. In the example provided, doing it "for the culture" means Black folks pushing up against the narrative that their linguistic system should be excluded from spaces where others deem it inappropriate. It also means acting in a manner that is liberatory to challenges in the environment. A simpler iteration: it can also mean wearing those Jordans to work with a suit, just "for the culture". This book is my version of doing it "for the culture" as I am speaking in both my authentic and academic voice. If this offends your sensibilities or pushes you to challenge or question my academic or intellectual ability to engage in this discourse, I'd implore you to ask yourself why and refer to "Chapter 1: Introduction" for some soul work.

What does this have to do with school culture, you ask? When I went through my own leadership program, I was taught that school culture is a subset of all the things a school leader is responsible for. In addition to school culture, a school leader is responsible for instructional core, mission and vision, capacity building, parent engagement, budgeting, and many other things. I propose an inversion of this idea. School leaders should do everything "for the [school] culture". School culture is the heartbeat of a school community and is, I believe, the most important part of leadership that should be used as the lever for impacting change in other areas. Need to adopt a new curriculum? Implement a professional learning plan? Have teachers volunteer for after-school preparation courses for students? Your school's culture will ultimately determine if these things are a success—and if your teams will endure through productive struggle—or if there will be an uprising of pushback and revolt. As a result, we should focus on how all of our decisions and potential outcomes impact the overall culture. The decisions we make are the roots of the tree, and the trunk is school culture. The leaves? Those are all of the outcomes and ways in which the culture is exhibited in the community. If the soil isn't nourished, the tree doesn't grow to its full potential. It may grow but will do so with whatever it is nourished with. Ultimately, we want to make sure we are providing nutrients that are best for what we desire. In the same way our bodies need protein, vegetables, and healthy nourishment alongside the occasional treat, schools need to be nourished and furnished with qualities that will help it thrive.

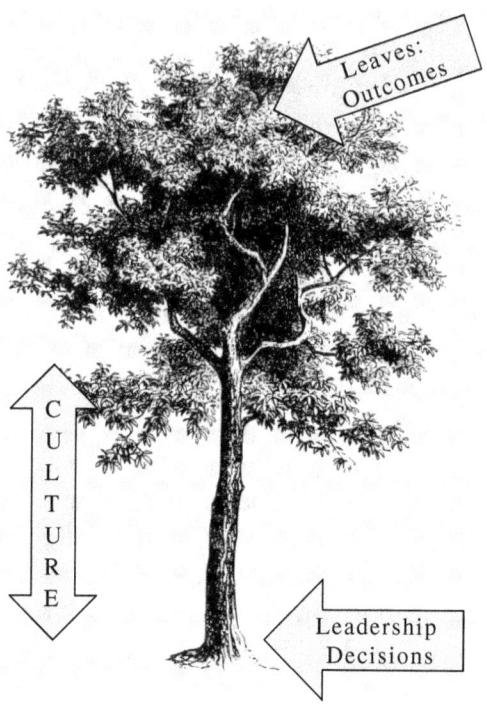

FIGURE 2.1 The "Tree" representative of the way your decisions impact the culture of your building. Whatever you feed the tree with at the roots will decide the culture, which then impacts the outcomes.

That is, what we decide as leaders becomes and supports the culture of the building. This translates to teachers, students, families, staff, and visitors. Therefore, we as school leaders have a responsibility to do everything "for the [school] culture". In a school, when stakeholders are doing things "for the culture", this means they are subscribing to the core tenets and values of the building in spite of their own momentary feelings and experiences. A willingness to endure even in the face of productive struggle is the ultimate goal and is an indicator of a strong culture. What would this look like in practice? Let's say there is a need for students to have their bathrooms painted because the conditions in the bathroom make it unwelcoming. The problem? There is not enough money in the budget to paint it. A culture driven by collaboration and shared responsibility will have teachers volunteer a few hours to help get it done or lead a team of students on the weekend to turn it into a community service project. Another example of this would be your wanting to implement a new after-school program that requires training during the day for staff. A culture where temporary disruption is tolerated will have this go off without a hitch. One where any change creates anxiety and friction will make this a nightmare. Before you can create or sustain a culture, we have some work to do with first assessing. "Test the Temperature" to evaluate the core values present in your community.

What Is School Culture and How Is It Impacted?

Before unpacking this inverted lens, let's first define *school culture*. There is ample scholarship and literature around "school culture" and most of it is oriented with the "subsect" ideology.

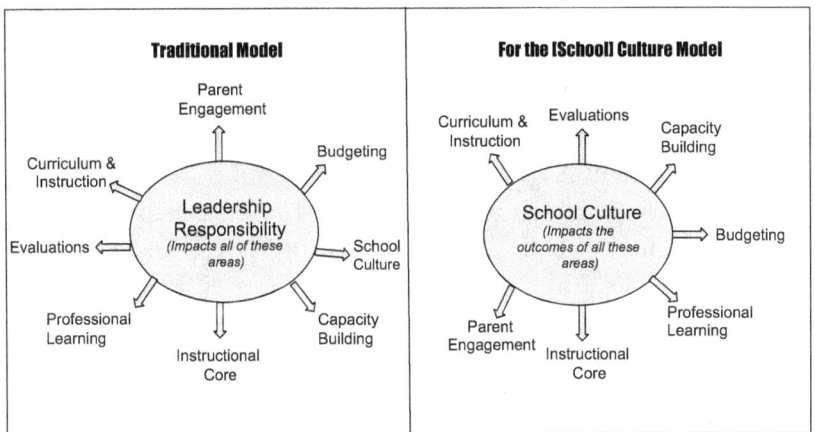

FIGURE 2.2 These figures represent the different models for school culture. In the traditional, school culture is a subset of the responsibilities of a leader. In the model I propose, the school culture determines the outcomes for all of the other areas, making it the nexus of a community.

TABLE 2.1 Test the Temperature

- Present a community challenge.
- Speak to impact/need/targeted outcome.
- Provide options OR ask for options or suggestions.

This means scholarship states school culture is its own area of school leadership that needs to be addressed. I believe the opposite. Your culture is summative and is a derivative of the decisions made daily that trickle down to staff, students, families, and the community at large. You can't just focus on building culture through community bonding and events. Culture needs to be nurtured daily through decisions.

School culture is also defined as the "feeling" you have when you walk into a school building. How are you greeted by office staff? Do the teachers all seem to be dragging in and loathing their assignments? Are students smiling and enthralled with their peers in the hallway? All of these can be informal indicators of a school's culture. Just like the example of the Black staff member using language or wearing clothing that is aligned with or indicative of their culture, staff and stakeholders in a school building are either supporting the culture present or pushing up against it with their actions, belief systems, and ways they engage within the community. For our purposes, *school culture* is defined as the norms, belief systems, and customs present in a school community exhibited through actions of stakeholders. It is important to note the difference here is that culture is impacted by the *actions* of the parties involved. As a school leader, you can declare a culture based on your expectations or vision, but it means as much as me declaring myself a millionaire. True evidence of culture is demonstrated only by how the building moves and functions on a daily basis. Taking that even further, a culture is consistently present. It is pervasive and exists in all spaces at all times. Students feel culture and it impacts everything from their learning experiences to their lunchroom interactions. Visitors feel the culture based on reception and engagement. Teachers' engagement with one another in collaborative planning is an indicator of culture as well as parent interaction in the community or lack thereof. If the culture is present only when there are visitors in the building, this is performative and is not truly a measure of how the building functions.

Each subsect in your building will also feel a culture of its own. Does the math team have more voluntary collaboration time than science? Does the parent engagement team work well or do only certain people mingle to engage in a project? To provide a deeper lens, Gruenert and Whitaker describe school culture by highlighting the differences between school culture and school climate. According to the authors, "if a culture is a school's personality, climate is its attitude. The biggest difference between the two is that an attitude is easier to change than a personality" (Gruenert and Whitaker, 2015). The assertion is that a school's climate will shift based on the changes and challenges present in the learning community—these shifts and fluctuations, though, will be temporary. However, a school's culture will remain the same even in the face of challenges as this is "how we do things around here."[1] I'd take it a step further and state a culture can be described as a school's "core values." While core values are the driving force behind a person's integrity and decision-making, the core values in a school are present in the ways stakeholders pivot and readjust after challenges present themselves. These challenges can come in the form of hiring decisions, a leadership turnover, student academic challenges, state shifts in requirements, and more. The decisions we make as leaders will have an impact on our community in ways that reverberate well beyond what we saw as potential outcomes. There will always be outside challenges that are an affront to a school's culture, and we have no control over them, so we should always consider those challenges, and our school's culture alongside them. Let's first talk through how your decisions shape the culture.

I offer the *"Head, Heart, and Hands"* model for culturally responsive decision-making to "do it for the [school] culture". The "Head" is the decision that needs to be made and the thinking that needs to go alongside it. The "Heart" is driving your decisions (head) based on your core values. The "Hands" are part of the decision-making process but are outside of the leader's control. It should, however, be considered in the process. By thinking of the "hands" part of decision-making, you are able to

TABLE 2.2

Head: *Thought Process*	Decision that needs to be made
Heart: *What do you value?*	Alignment with one's own values of leadership
Hands: *Boots on the ground (Result of Application)*	Potential impact of outcome of decision on school culture

examine the intent alongside the potential impact of decisions and how the decision will reverberate across the community. While decisions are often fast-paced and are "problem-solution"-oriented, focusing on the outcome allows for deep introspection about *how* things will be impacted.

An example is needing to hire a teacher two days before school starts because a teacher moved to another school last-minute. Do you hire the teacher with 20 years of experience who presents as a dogmatic pedagogue who may be unwilling to collaborate with newer teachers? Or do you hire the newbie who seems like they are open and willing to be molded? For each decision, there is a potential outcome that will prove challenging for the community. If you hire the seasoned teacher, you may have someone with deep content knowledge who is ready to teach without intervention right away. The potential challenge? They might be a turn-off to other educators in their community if they are oppositional or unwilling to collaborate and listen to the ideas of others. By hiring the newer, less experienced teacher, you will undoubtedly have some training to do. This will at first require a heavier lift from the teacher team supporting them. I'd argue that, in the long run, impact on the community will be better overall with the newer teacher. You are able to mold them and integrate them into the culture from the onset if you are intentional about the support and guidance they receive. You also are able to support the cultivation of their teacher identity aligned with the school's core value system. Instant gratification in decision-making may meet technical ends as a leader but often doesn't satiate overall. Quick decisions made absent of a process are akin to grabbing a banana instead of eating a full lunch. You'll be okay at first, but when hunger calls, that banana ain't cutting it. This leads to ravenous eating, which we all know causes unwanted outcomes. The result of using the formula is leaning into the process of making decisions with school culture exclusively in mind. Measure twice and cut once using the model. Here's an example of what can happen when you don't use your *Head, Heart, and Hands*:

TABLE 2.3 Head, Heart, and Hands in Decision-Making Example (Reactive): School Discipline

Challenge: Your data shows that students of color are being suspended at higher rates than their peers despite only being 25% of the school population. You decide to implement a restorative justice program to reduce suspensions for students of color but don't provide professional learning around the concept of restorative justice and only two staff members are trained.

Wondering: How could this well-intended system implementation adversely impact school culture?

Head
Decision: Implementing a Restorative Justice Program
Selecting a response to student discipline that is culturally responsive in nature and seeks to inform and shape behavior through positive intervention as opposed to punitive discipline

Heart
Core Values: Equity
Addressing disproportionate data for students of color through the implementation of a system that has the potential to create equitable discipline outcomes and teach life skills of building positive relationships and peer-to-peer engagement and discourse as well as repair harm caused to the community at large

Hands
Potential Impact/Outcome on culture:

1. There was no foundational learning around the history of the punitive nature of school suspensions and discipline for children of color. As a result, some staff may believe what is not true: "the students of color are being suspended at a higher rate because they are the only one's engaging in adverse behavior".
2. There was no professional learning for staff around what restorative justice is and its purpose. Therefore, there is no buy-in from those necessary to implement it.
3. Most importantly, there was no attempt to address the root cause of disproportionate data trends within the school building.

In the example above, the school leader was well intended and even attempted to implement a culturally responsive practice! We *should* use data to evaluate disproportionate outcomes and respond to them. Unfortunately, the leader did not use a model for decision-making beforehand, and we see the outcome is the lack of support for the program in the school community. We must understand that the "Head, Heart, and Hands" model should be used to work through a decision *before* moving to implementation. By doing this, we were able to see what steps the leader needed to take in order to ensure the system was truly supported before its roll-out to others. While this example shows how it can be used to assess the impact of the decision made after the fact, suppose the leader used the model before the implementation. This would have allowed them to determine that staff would need professional development to determine what the system is and why it's beneficial, ensured that staff were appropriately trained in the facilitation of restorative circles and conflict resolution, and allowed them to see they needed to get to the root cause of the disproportionality before deeming restorative justice as the solution. In this model, we are now able to implement actionable steps that support the decision by working backwards, but I would suggest using the model preemptively when making decisions so you are proactive versus responsive where possible. Let's work through a decision that is proactively using the model versus reactively:

TABLE 2.4 Head, Heart, and Hands in Decision-Making Example (Proactive): Grading System

Challenge: Student surveys show they do not feel challenged but are also indicating they don't understand their coursework. They also stated they are not motivated and care only about their report card grades. Teacher surveys show they believe students do not have an intrinsic value for education anymore and they are struggling to grasp grade-level concepts.
Head *Decision: Building student skills while creating intrinsic value in their learning through changing grading system* There needs to be a system present for students to gain understanding of the material being presented without seeing this work as a means to an end through report card grades. Mastery-based grading will allow for students to attain skills and focus on their proficiency versus numerical grades. This will be clearer for teachers to follow as well and is task- and standards-aligned.

(Continued)

TABLE 2.4 (Continued)

Heart
Core Values: Critical thinking and student engagement
Students should matriculate with attainment of grade-level skills as the driving force for their learning. They should have clear criteria and understanding of what skills they possess and what their growth areas are in order to improve and work on them. This builds independent learners and student accountability.

Hands
Impact/Outcome on Culture:
Changing the grading system will prove to be a challenge as shifting from numerical grades means that teachers will have to learn about mastery grading and determine what it will look like for their department. In addition, there is some mindset work as teachers are indirectly taught they are the arbitrators of student grades. Moving to an equity-driven system that does not allow for arbitrary grading will require professional learning and unlearning about the role of grades. Families and students will also need an understanding of the stem and how it impacts report cards.

In the example above, the leader used school data in the form of informal surveys and grades and determined there needed to be a shift in culture around grading and student engagement. The leader is able to determine that they want students to matriculate with a deep understanding of their own academic ability aligned with learning targets as a form of self-advocacy. More importantly, the leader was able to ascertain what steps needed to be taken and with what groups to help the decision be supported in its integration. While the leader cannot control how people will ultimately feel about the shift to mastery grading, they can rest assured they provided layered opportunities for support, learning, and implementation. The hope is that your culture is one that will support versus derail this initiative.

It may seem premature to discuss how culture is impacted before providing a framework for developing it, and for those who are taught that school culture is one part of a school's tenets for successful functioning, this is true. It is difficult to critique a system that you do not know how to establish. However, this model does not ask us to put the cart before the horse. If we consider each of our decisions and how they align with what we want the outcomes to be for our school building, the culture will develop itself. Much like a teacher who uses a lesson plan to determine what the students should learn or the outcome of the lesson, we have to drive our decisions on the basis of the school culture outcome we desire. If we equate this model to a lesson plan—shout out to all our fantastic educators—our core values as leaders are our standards and the learning targets are the outcomes we desire for our culture to be defined. Our decisions serve as the model or mini-lesson we use to *TEACH* how to reach the learning target. (Like how I did that? All of my expensive teacher training finally paid off!)

TABLE 2.5 Teacher Version versus Leadership Version

Teacher Version	Leadership Version
Lesson Standards =	Core Values
Mini-Lesson =	Decisions
Learning Targets =	Outcomes

Leading the decision-making process with our Head, Heart, and Hands in mind allows us to create culture daily while being mindful of those who will ultimately subscribe, unsubscribe, or derail the culture depending upon their own head and heart. This inverted model of school culture and decision-making will allow space for anxiety and uncertainty to be calmed or at least worked through. Should every decision be made using this model? Yes, where possible. Is this 100% going to ensure that as a leader you achieve the intended outcome? Of course not. I would argue, though, that inaction, or action without a process to think and reflect *before* action, creates large craters which will require more decisions. The worst outcome is potentially having to reverse a great decision that was made because it was not given all of the frontloading and support it needed to thrive. There will be scenarios where this model in its entirety is not applicable, and in those scenarios, you should use the parts of the model that you can. As an example, decisions as a school leader might have to be made rapidly. My suggestion is to always lead with your core values and reflect on the potential outcomes. All decisions you make as a leader impact school culture, even those that seem like they shouldn't, and this is why it's important to think of the outcome.

Here's a simpler example where a small decision can have an adverse outcome on culture. A staff member discloses a medical ailment to you that makes it hard for them to walk long distances for a few weeks. As a leader, you decide to give them your parking spot temporarily as it is close to the building. To the staff member, you are kind and thoughtful. To other staff, you are potentially showing favoritism. In my model, you used your Head and Heart to determine what mattered to you in that moment: the safety and comfort of the staff member in need.

TABLE 2.6 Head and Heart Challenge

Challenge: Staff member in need
Head: I am in a position to help, so I should.
Heart: Empathy, Kindness, Community
Hands:
♦ *From others*: Claims of favoritism; gossip   ♦ *From staff helped and others*: Kindness, humility

Will the culture be impacted by this singular decision? More than likely not. The streets will buzz, and you may even be asked about it. That's okay! For a culture to be disrupted once established takes recurring instances or decisions that the larger community does not agree with or does not have an understanding of. If the only people you gave up your parking spot to were staff members who agreed to pick up your dry cleaning and your order from Starbucks, *that* is a pattern that threatens positive culture. You don't want to know what the streets will say about that one!

Head, Heart, and Hands are interdependent. One impacts the other, and when the Head or Heart is not present, the Hands are directly impacted in a negative way. This is when perception is impacted and culture shifts. There will also be scenarios where you use your head and heart to make a decision and you have an adverse outcome or reception no matter how thoughtful you are. The idea is that so long as you do what's best for the community and are driven by your core values, you are on

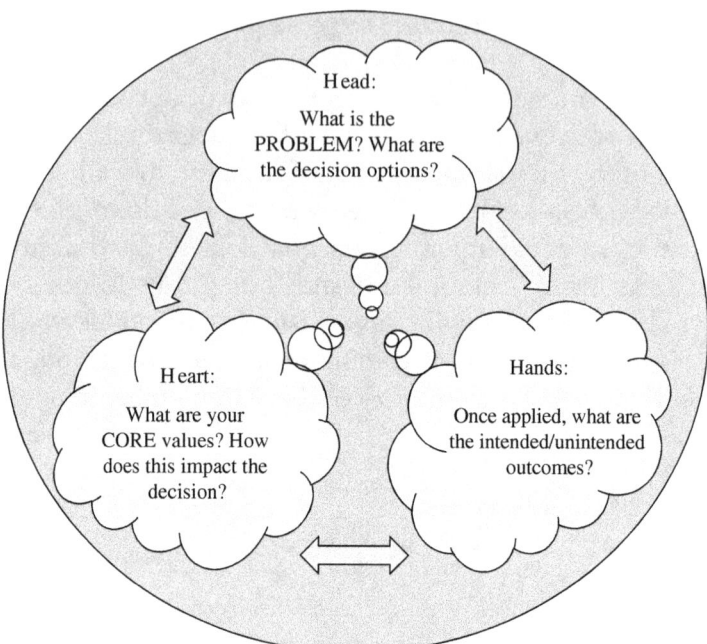

FIGURE 2.3 The "Head," Heart," and "Hands" are all dependent on one another. Without reflecting on one of these areas in your decision-making process, you run the risk of making a decision that will have adverse impacts on school culture.

the right track as a leader. The "Hands" of the strategy are contingent upon many factors. This includes your administrative team, district support/involvement, and most importantly the stakeholders in your building. As we will see in later chapters, it will be important to include and lean on these supports as a scaffold for ensuring your "Heart" and "Head" are reflected in the building.

Are you a skeptic who says you don't need a formula to drive your decision-making? Great! I love challenges. Here is an exercise for you:

Thought Exercise:

- → Think of a decision you've made as a leader that did not have a positive outcome or did not meet the intended outcome.
    - ♦ What were the obvious options at the time of the decision?

- What were options that you now know were available that you didn't before?
- Why did you make the decision you did?
- What was the outcome for the community? For yourself?
- Looking back, how would applying the model have helped?
- Did you make the decision because it's what made you feel good at the moment?
  - That is, did it feed your hubris? Temporarily quell your anxiety? Allow you to feel like a "boss"?
- What values drove the decision?

The inverse of being a thoughtful leader driven by values is being one who makes impulsive, rash decisions piloted by the worst parts of our human reactions: fear, anxiety, anger, and hubris amongst others. You will never regret thinking through a decision and having a rationale for why you made it. What I can promise is you will regret acting on impulse or without forethought as this can destroy a culture at a much faster rate than you can repair one.

Add Some Seasoning to the Formula: The Culturally Responsive Head, Heart, and Hands

Anarchy keeps things interesting, so here's the fun part. You can use the formula above and not be culturally responsive! It is extremely important to note while everyone operates from their core values, not all leaders realize their core values are not aligned with culturally responsive outcomes. Being culturally responsive as a leader is similar to being a culturally responsive educator as the tenets are the same. As a culturally responsive leader, you are assessing the needs of your school community on the basis of and inclusive of race, socio-economic status, and your own cultural competence (Diller and Moule, 2005). You are then using this knowledge to make decisions that factor these needs into your planning. You are also seeking to advance the success of stakeholders in various areas, including their own cultural competence and equity-driven lenses as these will ultimately positively impact the school community. For culturally responsive educators, there is an explicit focus on academic success for students alongside the tenets of socio-political consciousness and cultural competence.[2] There are current rubrics in circulation that speak to culturally responsive leadership, but it is important to understand that one's cultural responsiveness shows up in the decisions made daily that impact the school community and is reflected in how the community responds to those decisions. Before this takes place, one needs to examine their own willingness to be culturally competent. If you are in need of support in this area or would like to lead with love and are willing to explore and have not read this book in order, Chapter 2 is for you! Making a decision or having the ability to control outcomes does not make you a leader. Thinking deeply and proactively about who is impacted and how the decision lands makes you a leader. If you're making decisions that satiate you but leave the community starving, you have to look inward about what you truly desire in your role.

What is one to do if their leadership core values are not rooted in equity and cultural responsiveness? And how will you know? That is, a leader is making decisions based on their "Heart" but it does not align with what's best for a school community, for children of color, for families in need, and so on. If I were answering "for the culture," I'd state these people should not be leaders. If you are operating from a space that seeks to make decisions for children and a community but you "don't see color", "treat everyone the same," and aim for a community of assimilation rather than exploration and affirmation, the need is beyond a formula or framework for school culture. However, as an author who cares deeply about the hearts and minds of those taking care of our babies in schools, I will apply my own model here to demonstrate how it can be used to call in and support those who are in charge of making decisions but do so from a dogmatic or ignorant space. The model can be used to think through how to support someone who may be well intended but needs to develop their cultural competence and ability to reflect on their own heart.

TABLE 2.7 Thought work: Head, Heart, and Hands

Problem: A colleague says they are "equity warriors" but in meetings says very insensitive things (seemingly unaware) regarding students with learning challenges.

Head: My options are to use a cycle of inquiry to find out what their core values are that drive their decision-making *OR* call them out and tell them they're wrong.

Heart: My own core values tell me to use empathy and patience with this process as everyone's core values are driven by their socialization and lived experiences (even though I am uncomfortable with the language). My initial want is to call them out and tell them about themselves.

Hands: Intended outcome is for the person to self-reflect and/or take an approach that is responsive to the different genders, ethnicities/races, and plights of the students, children, and families in their building. In order to do this, I need not to call them out as this will cause them to shut down and disengage, but instead I need to provide space for discussion.

In the example above, it is very easy to name and call out someone else's problematic behavior. While this feels great in the moment and temporarily addresses the colleague's language, it does not get to the root cause of the problem and that is their mindset. If this person works with young people and you call them, out all you've ensured is that they'll avoid you or speaking their mind. The language and behavior will not change and that is the opposite response of what we'd want. If the person is comfortable saying these problematic things in front of adults, you can almost be certain these beliefs show up in their teaching practices and relationships with students. We want individuals to be able to speak their minds in spaces as you can't discuss, disrupt, or challenge a mindset you never hear. Instead, we should strive to lean into the better, more difficult parts of ourselves and use the model to be a support and shift hearts and minds. This is not easy. I have found myself and still sometimes find myself having to retract my word vomit driven by my initial, guttural feelings about problematic comments. The goal is to be reflective and think about the outcome and focus on the long-term goal, not my temporary feelings. I have also been on the receiving end of being called in with love even when I might not have deserved it. However, it allowed me to reflect and check myself versus defend and shut down.

Ultimately, it is important to acknowledge that school culture is an amalgamation of many different factors, some of which a school leader inherits or inadvertently cultivates. Operating from a space of cultural competence and knowing what we desire for our culture to be, as well as who is impacted based on the decisions being made, allow for a leader to be strategic and asset-based with their thinking and actions. Being a leader in any capacity is a high-stress scenario, but grounding your feet in what's best for your community, driven by a deep understanding of who you are and the potential impacts, ensures that even decisions that have unintended consequences—because we won't always get it right—won't leave you with the aftertaste of deep regret.

You Need Soldiers!

It is also important to note that the formula should not be a hindrance to actually making a decision. Culture is shaped by inaction just as much as the wrong action. When you make decisions, ask yourself who will keep their ears to the streets and will follow up on questions or concerns that arise. For example, what is being said in different departments about the system or structure you implemented? Who will talk to staff, students, and families about how the system is working? Did your decision provide a band-aid to a challenge or was it a real long-term solution? Are there additional needs to ensure that the decision reverberates in a positive way? These are all questions to consider after decisions are made to ensure that there are layered supports for wherever the chips fell. To achieve maximum buy-in and truly measure potential impact, you should provide as many opportunities as possible for stakeholders to engage in the decision-making process with you. Decisions made in isolation can lead to there being unintended consequences as we all have blind spots. We can't consult others for every decision, but where we can, this proves powerful and creates buy-in. In the examples with the implementation of the new grading system or restorative practices consulting staff about potential challenges, their opinion or prior knowledge on the systems, as well as finding out what the overall vibe is about a change in general, can be telling about your culture. As a culturally responsive leader, you will find that transparency is your wingman, and when you speak to why a decision was made and the intent behind the decision, you will at minimum provide a space for inquiry and understanding, thus illustrate humility over hubris. This is the difference between "I'm the boss, I don't have to explain anything" versus "Here's what I hope for and I'd like your partnership". The latter of the two is much more palatable.

"For the Culture"
Application and Materials

	Head, Heart, and Hands Decision-Making		
Entering	Emerging	Applying	Deepening
I understand the importance of making decisions for my community. As the leader, I make decisions objectively with the information I have available at the time.	I understand the importance of making decisive decisions for my community driven by school goals. I make decisions based on the moment and think about impact overall.	I make decisions and am transparent with my community about my rationale behind the decision being made. My core values are present in my decision-making, and I use my "head" and "heart" to inform my decisions.	Where possible, I seek/solicit input and feedback from stakeholders to inform my decision-making. My core values are present in my decision-making, and I also think through the impact on subgroups in my community thorough use of the "Head, Heart, and Hands Model".

Activity

Decision-Making—School Culture Activity

You know who you are as a leader! (If you aren't sure, read Chapter 1.) It is now time to think about how these values show up in decisions you will have to make daily. Before engaging in the practice activity, answer the questions below to determine how much of yourself you are bringing to your role as a leader.

Inquiry and Investigation

1. When you make decisions in your personal life, do you do so alone? With the support or thought-partnering with another? Why?
2. If faced with a difficult decision that you know will have unfavorable outcomes for some, how does this make you feel? How do you address it? Do you talk to others about it in advance?
3. Do you lead daily with your head and heart as the driving force? (i.e. belief systems and core values)
4. Rate your level of "cultural competence." Where do you fall? How will you move forward to improve or deepen?

Scenario-Based Practice:

Take it to the streets: Scenario-Based Preparation

Activity 1: Think of how you can apply the "Head, Heart, and Hands" model to an important decision in your personal life. Example: You have to tell a friend something they are doing is making you uncomfortable. What people do you consider with this decision? How will they be impacted? Where do your core values show up in how you will impact the culture of your relationship?

Activity 2: You have been principal for quite some time and realize that the core values of the school community no longer speak to the culture of the building. The core values were created over 15 years ago, and the students and staff no longer know what they are. As a result, they don't live and breathe in the community. You want to establish new core values that reflect the community you desire to have as well as those you serve.

So you want to "Lead"?
Get into this 'Literary' Work!

Notes

1 See chart on page 10 of "School culture rewired" Gruenert, S., & Whitaker, T. (2015). *School culture rewired: How to define, assess, and transform it.* ASCD.

2 For a deeper dive, see Dr. Gloria Ladson-Billings's Framework in Ladson-Billings (1995).

References

Alim, H. S., & Smitherman, G. (2012). *Articulate while Black: Barack Obama, language, and race in the U.S.* Oxford University Press.

Diller, J. V., & Moule, J. (2005). *Cultural competence: A primer for educators.* Thomson/Wadsworth.

Gruenert, S., & Whitaker, T. (2015). *School culture rewired: How to define, assess, and transform it.* ASCD.

Ladson-Billings, G. (1995). But that's just good teaching! The case for culturally relevant pedagogy. *Theory into Practice, 34*(3), 159–165. https://doi.org/10.1080/00405849509543675

Smitherman, G. (1996). *Talkin and testifyin: The language of black America.* Wayne State University Press.

Additional Reading

The Leadership Academy (n.d.). Culturally responsive leadership: A framework for school & school system leaders. https://www.leadershipacademy.org/resources/culturally-responsive-leadership-a-framework-for-school-school-system-leaders/

3

School Culture and Shared Values

What's the V.I.B.E.?

You became a school leader and before you stepped into the role, you automatically had an idea of what your ideal community would look like. From the facade of the building to the hallways and your office, you saw it all. Starting as a teacher, I always adorned my classroom in the way I wanted my students to feel when they walked in. There were representations of my own identity such as favorite authors and musicians, but there were also representations of what my students told me they wanted to see. I, of course, also did what was best for my type-A mental health by color-coding and placing things in an accessible way that made sense. When I transitioned to leadership, I had the honor of being hired in the community where I taught, so my expectations were realistic. I knew the challenges that presented themselves as well as what was needed in terms of small technical things I desired. I did, however, have a bucket list of things I needed for my office. I purchased organizers and copious amounts of regalia, bright-eyed and eager to organize myself and have the neatest space to work from. Then the school year started. Reality hits like Mike Tyson and suddenly all my expectations came crashing down. Then, my anxiety kicked in. Did I have my pretty, Pinterest-inspired office? Yup. Did that help me with doing my job and keep me organized? 25%. Having expectations is a normal trait. We all desire things to be within alignment with who we are and what we think is best. The challenge lies in the fact that being a leader, and specifically a school leader, initially has nothing to do with what we desire or expect. We have to go through a process of assessing and reflecting before addressing. We do this through reconciling with what we desire and what we currently have. I call this assessing for the V.I.B.E.

Reading the Room: Be a Prepared Visionary

Every community is an amalgamation of its inhabitants and their shared desires or lack thereof. A school is no different. There are teachers and staff members with varying roles, levels of involvement, and different lived experiences. There are students of various racial groups as well as age differences and home lives. As school leaders, we have to first detach what our "ideal" version of a school community is while still trying to find ways to imbue the community with a shared value system. This system should be reflective of your own core values around students and their experiences. (See Chapter 1 if you are unsure of what your core values are and if they are in need of disruption.) The value system should also include the voices of those who are part of the community.

Once you have your core values, you can jump straight into a two-page mission and vision outlining all the technical things your school will do, right? Wrong. It's easy to walk into a space and immediately list things you'd like to see happen or run off a list of deficits. It's another challenge to be strategic about your vision and assess what you already have that can be leveraged. Let's first create our working definition for "assessment". Assessment is defined as any sort of measure that can be used to determine the effectiveness of something else. In education, assessments are a measure of efficacy for a teacher, program, or resource and this will be discussed at length in Chapter 7. However, when it comes to the assessment of something such as a school community, we are defining the community based on what attributes are present and which are not. For the purposes of this chapter and our work moving forward, we will define *assessment* as objectively auditing for the purposes of determining elements present and/or lacking. In the case of a school building, we can assess school culture based on things we see and hear. What do hallways look and sound like during transitions? How do students and staff interact with one another? What programs, if any, are available for students as extracurriculars? All of these questions allow you to determine what a community has and what could be added. Before thinking of what we want to add to a community, we must first determine the baseline.

What does a V.I.B.E. require? First, one must be objective and assess from a lens that is asset-based. This is a challenge as people are already trained to see things based on how they meet or do not meet our needs and expectations. An example of this is walking into a community and saying the sports program is lacking because you always envisioned tennis in a school, despite the fact that there are six other sports offered. An objective assessment of a school community requires evaluation of what exists in the space already. Not whether what exists is good or bad aligned with our own values, just what is presented. This seems counterintuitive but it is extremely important for us to first remove our expectations and personal desires from the "assessment" process. Being driven by our expectations as we are assessing initially creates a gap that may not exist. We are then trying to fill that gap with what we'd like to see. Let's say you are evaluating a lesson for an educator you supervise. They have a strong content knowledge, encourage discourse with a protocol students are using, and seem to be excited about what they're teaching. The kids seem uninterested but are respectful. If you assess the teacher objectively, you'd note that their lesson was solid, they are deeply engaged in their pedagogy, and they seem to value student voice as there was a system created for it to thrive. If you are assessing with your own teaching expectations in mind, you may be looking for the teacher to teach the way *you* taught versus how they are comfortable. The danger in this is there may be no clear benefit to the teaching you would like to see. There might also be areas of improvement more glaring that the teacher needs to address. In this example, teaching like you is also not a task that would change the outcome for students. Simply stated, if you are evaluating the taste of a red velvet cake, it should be based on the critical elements of what a red velvet cake should have. Is the color on point? Are the texture and density appropriate to the cake? Does the sweetness fall in line with others or did they add something outrageous like nutmeg? If we are attempting to evaluate the cake based on the recipe grandma handed down that is your absolute favorite, anything else will pale in comparison.

For all of you thinking, "What does this assessment have to do with being culturally responsive?" Anyone can critique and evaluate as this requires only noticing what could be and what is not present. Critiquing often comes with no accountability and is just naming what you notice. To be an administrator, you *have* to be a dreamer as your job outcomes depend on your seeing all possibilities, but you are also responsible for being practical about how to achieve the ends you desire. I implore you to reflect on whether you are seeing the "glass half empty" versus "glass half full". As a teacher, I remember noticing many of my students were extremely unkind to their peers when they answered questions incorrectly. I knew they all struggled with something different but understood they would never name it and were all in need of confidence. The lashing out at others was a defense mechanism for what they saw as their own shortcomings. That is, if I'm pointing at others, no one is looking at me. As an activity, I asked them all to anonymously free-write things about themselves they admired. I then asked them to do the same for things they disliked about themselves. Each student had a list of indictments against themselves but struggled to speak about things that made them dope. I used this experience to speak through the power of mindset and how we are wired to notice what's lacking versus what's present that can be leveraged, celebrated, or even developed. The same is true for being a school leader. A school leader who is not culturally responsive will easily lean into their default of seeing deficits and what they would "do differently" absent of knowing the challenges presented, previous experiences between students, staff, and families, and the needs that *are* being addressed. The culturally responsive leader is a visionary who will assess the community by observing, asking questions, and listening. Before attempting to impart one's vision, the culturally responsive leader will ask themselves and others, "What's the Vibe?" Below is a tool for assessing just that. While there are different areas that can be assessed for the sake of specificity and a whole-school picture, use the framework below for an overall assessment.

TABLE 3.1 What's the V.I.B.E?: School Culture Edition

- *V (Voices) of the community*
- *I (Instruction & Interactions)*
- *B (Blessings)*
- *E (Environment (Physical Spaces & Transition/Feeling)*

V.I.B.E. Model for Assessment

What is V.I.B.E. exactly and why are we using it as an acronym? The term "vibe" is a word used to describe a feeling—that can have both positive and negative connotations in social situations. As an example, if I went to a family gathering and all of my favorite members were there, I may describe the event as a "vibe" because it brought about good feelings and positive energy. However, if that aunt showed up who always asks when I'm having more kids or spreads gossip, the "vibe" would be the exact opposite. The term can also be interchangeable for simply determining what the feeling is in general. This would sound like "What was the vibe of the meeting?" or "Your vibe seems off today—you good?" In either case, a V.I.B.E. is an energy that can be felt and described. While we can definitely feel the vibe in a school community, it is our job as school leaders to be able to name the attributes and factors that contribute to it as a measure of cultivating the V.I.B.E. or disrupting it. This is part of the assessment process. Let's first walk through each of the letters for V.I.B.E. as it relates to school culture. We can then use this assessment to develop or support a school's shared values.

V (Voices and Interactions)

There are a variety of voices in the school community that contribute to the way it functions. All stakeholders should be part of the conversation, and a "stakeholder" is anyone in your building who contributes to how it is perceived or how it functions. These are also the "streets" that determine the outcomes of the culture. In order to determine what a school needs, everyone's voice needs to be heard. The list of those to speak with can be exhausting, and before we talk about *what* to ask, we have to know *whom* to ask. Table 3.2 provides a list of every group in

TABLE 3.2

Take it to the "Streets"
❏ **Students**
❏ **Teachers**
❏ **Parents/Families**
❏ *Office Staff*
❏ *Custodial Staff*
❏ *Cafeteria Staff*
❏ *Safety Agents*
❏ *Neighboring Community Members*
❏ *Support Staff*
❏ *Administrative Team*
❏ *Leadership Team*
❏ *Community Members (partnerships)*

the building you should listen to as a measure of assessing your building. Though not exhaustive, it provides a lens into who the people are who contribute to the way your building functions and its overall vibe. Specifically speaking, things that each of these groups experiences and how they contribute to the environment are both revealing. For example, if you make it a point to interview the cafeteria staff and they state that none of the teachers ever comes down or they don't know who the school administrators are, that can be indicative of there not being a warm and welcoming culture for support staff. Should the cafeteria staff know every teacher in the building? Probably not, as teachers are not often in the cafeteria daily due to the nature of their work. Should they know some teachers and the names and likenesses of the administrative staff? Absolutely. Having a rapport with the cafeteria staff is a sign that, as a leader, you are invested in supporting and listening to the needs of everyone, not just those who are considered pedagogues. Another example why you should hear different voices in your community is to gain different perspectives about what happens or does not happen in smaller teams or spaces where you are not always present. An example would be the custodian knowing the teachers who always leave their room a mess versus the teachers who require their students to keep a clean space at the end of the day. Including student voice in the assessment allows you to hear how different teachers are received, if school programs are pleasing and effective, if they feel safe in the building, as well as what else they'd like to see in the future. Including educator voice in the assessment allows you to hear what the differences are in teacher experience, how different teams are run (math versus English, for example), as well as what teachers believe the "vibe" of the school building is. This is evidenced through subtle things like their expectations around their classrooms, collaborative work with their peers, and even support of the administrative team and new initiatives. Including the voice of support staff ensures they are also sharing their experiences from how parents and families are supported to the daily interactions between staff members in shared spaces. The most important voice needed for your assessment? The haters. These voices often present valid critiques and questions that can elicit positive change or be used to evaluate a system and structure that needs improvement. (For all those in their academic bag, "haters" are "dissenters").

I (Instruction and Interactions)

Just as important as what stakeholders are saying and doing in your building is what is being taught. Schools are often told what they have to teach, but *how* it is taught can be just as telling as *what* is taught. The instruction in a school community is more than the curriculum; it is also the educators' affect and their delivery of the material. In classrooms, something as simple as ensuring that a challenging topic has a "trigger" warning for students can be an indicator of a school culture where teacher's center student experiences in the classroom. In the interim, a classroom where a teacher's personal views become the forefront of a topic over student discontent and viewpoints can demonstrate a need for more teacher support or training on socio-emotional learning and student-centered approaches to building community. Speaking specifically to curriculum, you can assess if it is being taught from a culturally responsive lens, one in which there are different voices and experiences highlighted, or if teachers are simply following the "script" provided that centers one dominant narrative. Both of these perspectives can suggest what the school culture is around teaching and learning for students.

Curriculum is often reduced exclusively to what is taught in classrooms, but there is much more learning in a school than Science and Social Studies. It is also important to assess supplemental programs in the school community or lack thereof. Is there a curriculum for socio-emotional learning? Restorative Justice Program? Mentoring? After-school program? Assessing the instruction and curriculum of all these areas will not only allow you to see the quality of programs but also will help you understand if there is support for students outside of content they learn in classrooms. This will help you determine if programs are aligned with the school's instructional programming. This is important as a school building and its inhabitants should not just be centered on learning academic skills. You are also responsible for teaching social skills and developing citizens who can contribute to their community at large. You're in the business of "people building" and I don't know about you, but I'd like my future doctor to have social skills and humility, show kindness, and have the ability to problem-solve with an equity-centered lens. Again, it's important to note we are just assessing from the lens of what is present, not what is lacking—that comes later.

A wise woman once said, "students don't learn from people they don't like" (Pierson, 2013). This is true in any profession but is truer in no place more than a school building. Interactions and relationships are important and can illuminate unspoken challenges. In the example above, if students are reading Art Spiegelman's *Maus*—a graphic novel about the Holocaust—and a scene makes a student uncomfortable, a positive interaction would include the student informing the teacher of what they are feeling and the teacher responding in a way that is affirming and supportive of whatever the student needs in that moment. Taking it a step further, the culturally responsive teacher would surface the concern to the whole class and ask what students need to be engaged in a way that allows for difficult discussion but allows space for grace and respect (Arao and Clemens, 2013). This interaction, while subtle, is indicative of a positive classroom rapport and culture as students grapple with a topic that proves challenging but do so through the lens of learning how to engage with inequities and issues of oppression. Rather than veer away from difficult topics, educators should lean into these and teach students that discourse with varying viewpoints is part of life. Your school should be a model for how to engage in challenging topics with varied viewpoints.

Interactions with adults are also important to assess. Teacher meetings are a great place to take informal data. One can assess the willingness of staff to collaborate or engage with their peers. Do staff show up on time and ready to work? Does one voice dominate the meeting while others text and scroll through photo albums? Are some grading while others are tracking data?

Assessing and observing interactions outside of the teaching realm can also be revealing. For example, a parent walks into the main office and is not greeted by any of the staff. For the parent this one interaction, while simple, can suggest the staff is cold, standoffish, or not paying attention—none of which is positive for parents or families. Another great place to assess interaction? The hallways. What does a transition look like for students and staff? When students go to the bathroom or stop to ask for help, how are they treated? Do they talk to one another in a positive way? What do school yard or lunch room interactions look like? Do staff members talk to one another across grade? Department? Is the office staff friendly with teachers? Do the custodians interact with everyone? Standing back and assessing the interactions between community members—both spoken and non-verbal—allows you as a leader to determine the "temperature" of the building in different spaces and amongst different groups. This informal data is invaluable and requires nothing more than listening and watching. Non-verbal interactions are valuable sources of information and are a secondary data source after the "voices". In the example above, the "voices" can be used to unpack and understand some of the interactions and observations so as to not draw conclusions without more context. You can ask members of the community how they feel in different spaces and then use inquiry to unpack the non-verbal interactions noticed. Not listening to the voices alongside the interactions can be dangerous and allow for planning which does not address the root cause of challenges presented. To have a deep understanding of the interactions, you should always ask more questions by taking it to the "streets" to unpack what you've observed by listening to the Voices. Context, as well as pretext, is extremely important when evaluating interactions. Let's say you notice that two teachers in a meeting are texting one another and looking uninterested—evidenced by one person picking up their phone once the other puts theirs down (if you know, you know).

TABLE 3.3 Leaning into the Voices after an Interaction

1. I noticed....
2. It suggests....
3. I wonder....
4. Whom can I ask (Voice) to gain more insight?

This interaction, at face value, can suggest that the teachers are disengaged and not paying attention. Talking to one of them or using inquiry (Voices) in response to the observation instead might reveal that they believe their voices don't matter in the space based on previous experiences you were not privy to. This is a larger issue that needs to be addressed but might have been missed if you relied on the interactions in isolation. Both verbal and non-verbal interactions are necessary to evaluate a culture. Use inquiry to make sense of interactions that appear to present a challenge or speak to there being disruption in the V.I.B.E.

B (Blessings)

Each school community will have different budgets and this directly impacts the programs that a school is able to offer. Evidence of a well-developed school building is that it has programs for students, families, staff, and other stakeholders to extend learning or offer new learning opportunities. The offerings should be interwoven into the culture of the school building and should help build and support the systems that benefit the community. There should also be opportunities to just "vibe" and be in community with one another. This can be in the form of purposeful bonding opportunities between staff and students, amongst staff and students, and informal opportunities for being in community learning about one another. These come in the form of structured events. "Blessings" are anything in a school building that can be viewed as an asset due to its being able to leverage and support the overall school goals. These include things in school buildings that are not initially being seen as a "blessing" because they are in the infancy stages or need more development. Examples are new programs, courses, staff members, and more. Though in need of cultivation, these things are still assets and should be viewed as such because with the right development they will eventually have positive outcomes. Let's say, for example, you are assessing a school community and they have a restorative justice program. Through your investigation, you discover that many teachers have an understanding of what restorative justice is, there is some evidence of the practices being used as an alternative to punitive discipline, and there is staff trained in facilitation of restorative circles. There is room for growth as students and families do not have a shared understanding of restorative practices, and for true implementation, this is necessary. Despite the system's not being fluid in the school community, evidence of its existence is a blessing because it lays the foundational work to either continue the system, if it aligns with your ethos and core values for the community, or discontinue it by choosing not to develop or sustain its implementation. Blessings are evident in all parts of school culture. Some tangible examples are professional development opportunities for stakeholders to implement a system— curricular or non-curricular after-school programs aligned with school-day activities and supplemental support for extended learning. Another blessing that is often overlooked? Systems and structures for celebration amongst staff and in teams. Is there already a method for peers to acknowledge the success of one another or celebrate positive things happening in one another's lives? Does the community receive acknowledgment for collaboration and sharing their learning? If so, these are also blessings that should be cultivated and supported as adults are students in need of acknowledgment and celebration too! I mentioned budgets and their being leveraged to support the V.I.B.E. If used appropriately, finances may be a starting point to cultivating a vibe but should eventually waiver (see Chapter 4 for more on budgeting). Using your budget to create an environment where staff feels valued and becomes intrinsically motivated to celebrate leads to blessings as the acknowledgements and affirmation should naturally become part of the culture. If done well, staff should want to celebrate one another as well as students even when money to do so dissipates. The acknowledgment should become the driving force, even though everyone likes a little somethin somethin once in a while. It is important for you as a leader to understand that your budgetary decisions sometimes plant the seed that allows celebration to grow in your community. This matriculates to when you are not able to be part of it yourself. Be sure to take stock of what the community possesses already and always count your blessings!

E (Environment)

The most challenging part of assessing a school community comes from the feeling of the environment. Just like a V.I.B.E., the "environment" can be difficult to assess as it requires one to ascribe an objective attribute to something that is just a "feeling". In order to determine what the environment is *telling* us, we need to break it down into physical spaces, interactions, and feelings. Below are some questions to ask yourself, and others, as you are moving through the community as a starting point.

- *Physical Spaces*: What do classrooms look and sound like? Is there representation of various identities, learning styles, and levels of learners? Are bathrooms tidy and monitored? Are hallways kept clean and do students/staff take ownership of keeping it clean? (If there is

something on the ground, do people walk past it or pick it up?) Is there student work displayed that is more than grades? Are the school core values evident?
- *Interactions*: Are students and staff kind to one another? How do staff communicate with each other, administration, custodians, kitchen staff, and so on? Are there exchanges at all? What does the cafeteria look and sound like at lunchtime? What do transition periods look and sound like? What do team meetings look like? How does staff interact with parents? Do the administrators visit meetings and classrooms as regular practice? How are they received?
- *Feeling*: Would you want to be a student/staff member/parent in the community? Why or why not? Does the building feel *cold or warm*? What attributes make it feel this way? Stand near the timecards in the morning. Are teachers apathetic as they come into work? Do they talk to one another? What is the turnout for school events? Does staff exhibit pride in the community? Students? Can people speak to the school's values? Are there informal conversations between students and staff in common spaces?

You Have the V.I.B.E. Now What?

Being a culturally responsive leader requires us to step outside of our hubris and our desire to impart our own belief systems upon others. It is imperative to know who you are as a leader as well as what you believe is best for children given the community you serve. However, a leader is remiss if they don't ascertain what their community has and needs by listening to those who govern it every day. You're the "boss," sure. But your success depends wholly on the actions, beliefs, and attitudes of those you serve. A culturally responsive leader knows that being good at numbers, having extensive experience working with teams, and those all-alluring doctorate degrees mean nothing if they are not first willing to listen, be responsive to the needs of those who are boots on the ground daily, as well as determine what exists already that can be leveraged for supporting the community. The difference between being a leader in title and being one who is culturally responsive in assessing a community is glaring. The appointed "leader" will walk into a community and tell its members what it needs based on a conflated belief system. They will also seek to make changes in isolation in a building they have been part of for years and not think of the impact for those involved. The culturally responsive leader will determine the V.I.B.E. and use that to listen to and interrogate the community as a means of strengthening what is already strong and cultivating what needs water to grow. It is also important to note that the VIBE model is not just for assessment of a new community. I would argue that the model should be used for various stages of leadership as a vibe is capricious and can change as the school develops or evolves. Staff turnover, changes in leadership, integration of new curriculum, as well as requirements for teaching are all things that can impact the vibe of a school community. Use the model as you see fit when the need arises to "test the temperature" of a community. See the rubric that follows for a V.I.B.E. interrogation checklist to support this culturally responsive inquiry work. We assess for a V.I.B.E. as a measure of determining what values are present within the community. For there to be a V.I.B.E. you want to see thrive, there needs to be voice from all of those who are part of it. Your assessment of the community and the feedback you elicit supports the cultivation of school values everyone can get behind because they have been part of determining what they are.

The culturally responsive leader not only will interrogate using various data points but will reflect on the way their lived experience impacts their understanding of the data. If you are part of a community that is different from what you are accustomed to on the basis of your lived experience, there will be a challenge with interrogating the data as negative and unintentional mental models can skew *what we think* we see. For example, if I am not accustomed to a community of Black children where choral oration in the form of freestyle or playing the "dozens" (Smitherman, 1996) takes place and shows a sense of community, I may interpret this as a raucous interaction as opposed to one that is full of love and light! There is no removal of oneself from culturally responsive leadership, and it is important to consistently interrogate not just the communities we serve but also the interplay between our lived selves and those we show up to serve daily.

Honor, Cultivate, or Disrupt?

Since you are now an expert on how to determine a VIBE, how do you know when the VIBE is off? And what do you do about it? If all signs point to there needing to be disruption in the culture or at least part of the culture, it is your responsibility as the leader of the community to lead the conversation and name your observations. Ask the community why they think the VIBE is shifting, ask if your assessment is accurate, and what the contributing factors are. While you may not elicit honest and open responses by asking the whole community formally, asking in purposeful gatherings or through informal conversations will provide confirmation as well as additional information. Once you've decided to disrupt a VIBE, do so decisively and articulate why it has been uninvited to the party. While you can delicately obtain feedback and take an inquiry stance for assessment, there are times where the threat is so great you have to move with intention. Once something has undoubtedly been named a threat to positive VIBES, it has to go. You should explain why it has to go and lead this conversation with your core values and the negative impact to the community at the center of your discussion. This applies not just to the community at large but also to smaller teams. This presents challenges especially when sometimes the bad VIBES are your mindset and people you put in leadership positions. Yikes.

TABLE 3.4 Example: Bad Vibes

You've put your ear to the streets and discovered that one of your administrators has expressed discontent to staff about your desire to expand an accelerated program to all students instead of just those recommended by teachers. This is indicative of your leadership team not trusting you *or* not being comfortable being honest. The larger issue is that the person is exhibiting bad VIBES because they've inadvertently illustrated disconnect amongst the leadership team and the initiative. If this news spreads, the impact is resounding. Factions are a threat to culture and have to be disrupted without question.

In this case, you should take an inquiry stance with the administrator about the program and their feelings, NOT about the information you've obtained. You want to understand their heart and why they have an apprehension to expanding the program. Remember, the culturally responsive leader calls people in, not out, even when disruption is necessary. If the behavior continues, calling them out may be necessary, but note that this will cause further tension. In some cases, though, the tension is worth the outcome. How would you start this conversation? What steps would you take?

"WHAT'S THE V.I.B.E.?"
Application and Materials

What's the V.I.B.E.?
School Culture Edition

Entering	Emerging	Applying	Deepening
I understand school needs based on information provided by higher-ups or those on my administrative team.	I assess a school based on tangible data points as they are objective.	I assess a school based on multiple data points, including data, observations, and stakeholder voice.	I assess a school based on the triangulation of objective and subjective data points inclusive of stakeholder voice.
I value and respect positional authority.	I value objective sources of data as subjectivity skews information.	In addition to objective data, I value the voices of those at different levels and understand each person's opinion adds a different lens.	In response to data, I ask questions to challenge my own mental models and biases connected to my race and lived experience while unpacking noticings.

Activity

Are you a VIBE?

You are walking into a building and are eager to apply the V.I.B.E. model. Before doing this, assess the V.I.B.E. of your leadership by answering the questions below.

Mirror, Mirror on the Wall…

1. What is one word your family would use to describe you? Coworkers? Friends?
2. How would you describe your leadership style? How do you think this makes people feel? Are you comfortable leading in this way or do you desire to change? Why?
3. Are you a social person in your personal life? Professional? (You're in service of the people!)
4. How much of yourself (family, likes, dislikes, beliefs) do you share with colleagues?
5. If you walk into a meeting, does the energy shift? Why do you think that is?

Truth Serum…

1. Use the questions above and ask others! The best way to assess what your vibe is will be to ask others and be willing to accept the feedback. Get out of your feelings and into some growth!

Scenario-Based Practice:

What's the V.I.B.E.? Scenario-Based Preparation

You've used the V.I.B.E. model and have the data points below. What letter of the strategy is missing? What is your next step based on the data provided?

Data

- Students talk to one another in the lunchroom and seem to move about without cliques. Lunch transitions are noisy but safe and positive.
- Teacher teams intervisit with one another willingly (most people), and there are staff who signed up for training on peer mediation.
- Data shows that students who are learning English and a second language are scoring well below their peers in English language arts but are excelling in math based on state exam data.
- You heard a teacher say "What else did you expect" when a colleague said there were a lot of teacher coverages for the day.

What did I get myself into?!
Reads to get you thinking

Bibliography

Arao, B., & Clemens, K. (2013). *From Safe Spaces to Brave Spaces: A New Way to Frame Dialogue Around Diversity and Social Justice.* https://www.anselm.edu/sites/default/files/Documents/Center%20for%20Teaching%20Excellence/From%20Safe%20Spaces%20to%20Brave%20Spaces.pdf

Pierson, R. (2013, May 3). *Every Kid Needs a Champion.* www.ted.com. https://www.ted.com/talks/rita_pierson_every_kid_needs_a_champion?trigger=5s

Smitherman, G. (1996). *Talkin and testifyin: The language of black America.* Wayne State University Press.

4

Budgeting

What ya Pockets Lookin' Like?

As a child, I was fortunate to grow up in an environment where I didn't want for anything. My family wasn't wealthy, but we were comfortable, and I was able to do all of the things I wanted with friends and at school. I vividly remember, though, in high school, being told I did not qualify for free school lunch and had to pay for it due to my parent's income. Pay? For the gross gelatinous pizza and the burgers with the weird circles on them? Nah. This was the first time I thought about what my parents made and how that impacted what I was able to do, or not do, in school. Another thing I remember well was the difference between my private middle school experience and my public high school experience. With public schools depending on your region and/or state, funds vary greatly. One example of this disparity is New York State being the first in per-pupil spending while California is 22nd despite having much higher taxes than NY (Hahnel, 2020). This translates into New York City being able to offer things to schools that California cannot due to monetary costs such as professional learning to support teacher efficacy and support for varied learning needs. My private school was not the stuff you see on TV, but there were differences in the way the building looked, the courses and experiences we were offered, and the way we received communication from the school and the parish. There will always be disparities between public and private schools as the private advantage is often more funding due to tuition and enrollment. While public schools cannot control their funding, they can control how it is spent and whom it benefits.

Hiring Practices "Whose mans is this?"

School Staff

A large part of your budget will be assigned to your hiring and staff needs. Can't run a school without people, right? As needs vary from school to school, the squad should also look different. There are many roles to fill and each one is important for different reasons. You can blindly hire based on resume qualifications and first impressions, but I implore you to take inventory of what the school needs outside of licenses. Budgets are not the same year to year, and the driving force for your hiring or letting go should follow the most important need areas. The culturally responsive leader will ensure that first operational needs are met—safety, cleaning, and so on—and then will evaluate their student population to determine what *they* need in order for them to be taken care of. Let's work through an example:

- ♦ Your school population is as follows:
  - 40% special education
  - 20% students who are housing-insecure
  - 15% English as a new language/English language learners (ENL/ELL)
  - 35% of all students are at least two grade levels below in reading

Based on this makeup, I know I need at least someone to support the students who are housing-insecure, ENL/ELL teachers, and a reading interventionist *or* program to support literacy and reading comprehension outside of the core curriculum.

I will keep harping on this fact because it is the most important—the decisions you make should always be based on the make-up and needs of your community. Without this at the forefront of your budgetary decision-making, the potential impact cannot truly be measured. To consider what staff is necessary, you must assess the landscape. Of course, you need teachers, but there are other staff members who are just as important. Let's determine who they are:

- *Counselors*
  - Every school requires counselors regardless of age or demographic. The challenge lies in having an adequate number of counselors who meet the needs of your community. "Adequate" is, of course, a subjective term as the demand and needs will vary. At minimum, you should have a student-to-counselor ratio that allows for mandated students to be seen according to their schedule and for counselors to have additional time to address needs that arise from students who are not mandated. Another layer? You should also have your counselor(s) integrated into the community outside of their designated role. This can be through leading workshops for families and students, running/supporting clubs, or being available to work alongside the administrative team to plan for supports and interventions. One more thing! The language needs of the students/families in your community should be taken into consideration. Having a counselor who is able to connect and support by being bilingual or multilingual provides a sense of security and safety for those they engage with. Instead of having to rely on other staff members who speak the language to translate, starting with someone who is native to a specific culture or language is ideal. This shows thoughtfulness and allows for true immersion for families.
- *Social Workers*
  - School social workers are integral—if you can afford them, of course—as they are also guidance counselors who offer a deeper, holistic approach to the needs

of students *and* families. Whereas guidance counselors often focus on student needs and socio-emotional development, social workers are able to go a step further and support family needs or challenges that may impede or support the success of a student. An example scenario is a student who is new to the city and their parents are unfamiliar with supportive housing programs and how they can be accessed. A social worker will support the family through connecting them to the appropriate agencies and may even assist with applications. In addition to assisting the family, the student will be supported through their counseling in the school building. A social worker will also support families with outside referrals for counseling or support for students to provide a whole-family approach to support.

- *Support for Students who are Housing-Insecure*
  - In every state in the US, there are students whose families struggle with housing insecurity as well as food insecurity (Godoy, 2023; Chatterjee, 2024). Having a staff member specifically support these students, especially if you have a large population of them, is a no-brainer. These families are often in need of support not just with housing but also with food, clothing, and more. We know that stress at home can manifest itself in children through adverse behavior or withdrawal, and having them receive targeted interventions outside of school as well as inside provides a comprehensive support that best sets them up for success. Hiring a coordinator or designating a person to work exclusively with these students allows for a relationship to be built that is driven by support for the needs of students and families. The challenge is that you have to be able to pay for the position or designate someone who is already hired to work with this group. They should also have a yearly budget within the school's funding to be able to support what students and families need. Examples of things

that can be done with the funding are hosting events specifically for these students and families around holidays, providing clothing/uniforms for students, and paying for their inclusion in school events that may have a monetary cost. Oftentimes, these are the areas where families need the most support. Another layer of being culturally responsive is to simply ask families what their needs are and let them know you are willing to support them. Inquiry over assumption is your friend.

- *Teachers!*
  - Teachers are extremely important to a school building! What is a building without them?! They are the orchestrators of school culture as well as the ones students will be with the most throughout the day. As a result, you should make sure you have enough teachers to cover the program and provide quality, culturally responsive instruction. You should have qualified teachers for supplemental programs whether instructional or non-instructional in nature. Teachers cover a wide range of supports:
    - **Special Programmatic Needs**
      - Based on your population, there may be a need for teachers who are licensed in special areas. Examples of this are ESL (English as a second language)/ENL teachers. Another special license area is special education services. If you are a culturally responsive school leader and you have the student population to support the needs of these educators, the decision to hire them is non-negotiable. While you may not be able to hire a large number, their inclusion in the budget is necessary as a means of ensuring that students are receiving the services necessary to be successful. I'd argue you need them regardless of demographic designation as we've all taught students in need of varied academic support who were not identified as such.

- *Remediation*
  - In your program there should be teachers who can provide tailored intervention services for students in need. Do you have a population of students who receive special education services through alternate programming? Then you need teachers who can provide these services in various areas. Examples are math and reading. While classroom teachers are taught to do their best and provide instruction that addresses varied learning needs in their daily instruction, there should be teachers who receive training specific to the learning needs of students in various areas. These will sometimes be your special education teachers listed above but may also be someone who is specific for reading interventions or math interventions but who does not teach in a regular classroom setting. They would be exclusively for students who need a more targeted, small-group approach. This is not exclusive to your special education population. All classrooms have students in need of support academically, and oftentimes they are not designated as special education or needing language support. It is imperative that you have teachers who can address these areas of need as part of their department.
- *Acceleration*
  - Students and families are always looking for advancement opportunities in their school community. As the leader, you should always provide programs that can add value to a student's educational experience to extend their learning. Examples of this are Advanced Placement courses, gifted-and-talented programs, certificate programs, or even something as simple as a coding program as an

elective. The more opportunities you provide for students to engage positively and intellectually outside of their regular coursework, the more they will remain in the building and contribute positively to its culture. Of course, these programs require teachers who are licensed and certified and therefore come at an added cost. While you may not be able to afford these teachers specifically, you may have staff members who already have this license or a desire to obtain it. Showing support for this would build capacity amongst staff and is a blessing!

- **Extracurricular**
  - Often overlooked, clubs and after-school programming are an extension of the school day. If done well, they are the thing students most look forward to. In an ideal budgetary plan, students would have the opportunity to join clubs run by teachers or other staff members and they would align with student interests. Some examples are gaming clubs, art, book clubs, music creation, basketball, football, and content creation—the list can go on. You should ask students what they prefer for a tailored approach to clubs and enrichment, but they should be run and/or supported by teachers. This allows for a layered approach to relationship-building and provides the opportunity for students to show their brilliance in ways that are non-academic in nature. Teachers need to and deserve to be compensated for this. If your culture does not allow for this because staff are unwilling or just unable to stay, you can hire outside consultants, but this is not the same. Building relationships between students and teachers after school is money in the bank and allows them both to

share and shine at skills not always showcased during the day. If you simply can't afford it but have the support, try to integrate it within the school day. Even better, you can also plan to have a Community-Based Organization partner with your community for after school, and oftentimes they would have their own budget for programming. Aligning with them allows for a partnership and representation of the school's core values being displayed both during and after school. Parents and families often possess skills and talents that are beneficial to the community! Tapping into those resources and creating partnerships allow for distributive leadership and inclusion, showing that you value the community at large, not just those who work for you.

While I've just provided all of the ideal scenarios with hiring and programming, the harsh reality is that most budgets cannot sustain this, and this is where difficult decisions have to be made. How you make the decision will determine the impact on school culture. Not being able to afford things based on your budget just means you have to be strategic, but it is not an excuse to forgo being thoughtful about community needs. When you have to cut programs, you have to dive deeply into your culturally responsive tool kit. Impact should always be at the forefront of your decision, and the community needs are paramount. Here's practice:

TABLE 4.1 Head, Heart, and Hands in Decision-Making Example: Budget Crisis

Challenge: There is great opposition to the new adoption of a curriculum for the math department. Staff has expressed being overwhelmed, and they'd like support to understand it better before rolling out in classrooms. You cannot afford to hire consultants to come in and support.

Wondering: If the department does not receive support, how could this adversely impact school culture?

(Continued)

TABLE 4.1 (Continued)

Head
Decision: Supporting staff with implementation of a new curriculum

Teachers are asking for support to meet the goal of implementing new teaching material. This is actually a good place to be in as there is a willingness and cooperative nature associated with asking for support versus expressing discontent and opting out. Teachers have to be supported and have their request.

Heart
Core Values: Transparency and Community

Moving to support teachers is the right answer because they are ultimately using their learning to benefit students across the school community. You do want to show the department you heard them and want to meet their needs. You also need to communicate that there are no funds for outside support.

Hands
Impact/Outcome on culture:

1. As you have communicated there is no money for outside support or consultancy, this shows there needs to be a creative, in-house solution to the curriculum learning.
2. You suggest that a smaller team can work to "unpack" the curriculum and this can be turnkeyed to the department as a whole. This can be done by volunteers or by teacher leaders in your team.

In the example above, although the process may be slower, it will address the need asked for while addressing the budgetary challenge. It has also provided an opportunity for distributive leadership as the learning will happen inside the community which shows the experts are in the building versus coming in from the outside. The impact on culture here will be positive. Here's another example to work through:

TABLE 4.2 Apply the Head, Heart, and Hands Model

Challenge: You have an incoming 6th-grade class. Data shows they are at least two grade levels behind in math. You don't currently have a certified interventionist, and hiring one would require cutting a program for students or that new parent after-school book club. What to do?

Administrative Team

One of the most important aspects of school leadership is who is in charge. Aside from the principal being the face of the building, the administrative team is responsible for the messages communicated and for integration and support of school goals and are also boots on the ground for all things the principal may not be aware of. Assistant principals (APs) are the throughline between the principal and other stakeholders in the building. Without them, there would be chaos and civil unrest! As an AP myself, I am biased, of course. However, the reality is a principal cannot effectively run a school building with a team of administrators who are not like-minded in goals, leadership ability, and belief systems. This does not mean the administrative team needs to agree on all things and have the same leadership style. It does mean, however, the team needs to be able to have difficult conversations, support one another's ideas and initiatives, and share an affinity for the end goal—support and equity for student outcomes. How does this align with money and budgeting? You need to be able to afford APs! There are many things to oversee in a community, and the APs are the ones who divide and conquer to ensure that systems are being followed and the streets are getting what they need. They are necessary, though, because each handles specific things within the school community. If you cannot afford them, you should think equitably about distribution for what you have. Here's where the challenge comes in: are you able to sparse out the workload without sacrificing quality of the work being done?

Each school will have multiple subjects and teams to oversee. Ideally, each AP would be responsible for a team or grade as well as specific school-aligned initiatives. For example, an AP can be responsible for the English language arts/English department, the 6th-grade team, and parent engagement for the building. That would leave other departments such as math and science to have an AP oversee them as a means of ensuring that curriculum is aligned with state and district policies, engagement with students aligns with the ethos of the school, and teachers are being supported with any of their concerns. This includes the grading policies, needing additional support for students, and helping to engage with parents. This all sounds great until you assess the budget and realize APs are a luxury when they should be a necessity. Administrators are more costly in salary due to the supervisory nature of their role, and hiring one can equate to reducing a program for your school, not hiring that new elective teacher you needed, or getting rid of that Saturday program that kids loved so much—all as means of offsetting the cost of hiring. On the other hand, if you don't hire, who does all of the technical tasks associated with the role of AP? Evaluations, planning for school engagements, and keeping a tight hold on the school's instructional and socio-emotional goals. Unless you are the principal and plan to put the whole school on your back, you will need APs/vice principals to be ten toes down to support the school's goals.

As previously mentioned, APs, outside of just being there for technical purposes, are also there to serve adaptive ends which are shifting mindsets and working closely with the staff while keeping their ear to the streets. The AP's role is to keep all level-one challenges or concerns off of the principal's plate by addressing them or providing solutions. This work is often the most important yet unseen. Supervision becomes worth the money when your administrative team is able to execute the mission and vision of the school building while supporting the vibe of positive school culture. They are also responsible for supporting the cultivation of positive relationships in an environment rich in equity-centered instruction/relationships. But what is one to do when their budget says no to an AP but the environmental needs say yes? This is another perfect example where the Head, Heart, and Hands model can be applied. (Refer to Chapter 3 for deeper exploration of the formula.)

TABLE 4.3 Head, Heart, and Hands Model

Head: *Thought Process*	Decision you desire to make
Heart: *What do you value?*	Alignment with one's own values of leadership
Hands: *Boots on the ground*	Potential Impact of Outcome of decision on school culture

Let's walk through what this would look like both as the principal of a school and as the assistant principal (AP).

Scenario 1

♦ You are the principal of the school and have one AP overseeing two content areas. You are also spread very thin and have to conduct evaluations while supervising more than one team. You realize there is a need for another AP, but this would mean not adding the filmmaking program students have voted for.

Scenario 2

♦ You are the AP of the same school above and are in dire need of support. While you have been accustomed to overseeing multiple departments, you are not doing so effectively and are becoming burnt out. The principal suggests hiring another AP – at risk of not having the filmmaking program – or having a teacher already in the building teaching a smaller program.

TABLE 4.4 Principal Challenge: Hire Another Assistant Principal (AP) or Reduce Program?

Principal Challenge: Do you hire another AP at the cost of reducing or cutting the program?

Head: Thought Process	**Decision you desire to make:** *Your AP has confided in you about being overwhelmed and not being able to effectively support the community. They are pulled into many directions and are masters of none. This is counterproductive to the community goals. The filmmaking program is equally important as you desire to add a program that prepares students for the 21st-century skills. Students have also voted for this program.*
Heart: What do you value?	**Alignment with one's own values of leadership** *The core values here are communication, transparency, and student voice. Various stakeholders have expressed their needs, and you value their voices.*
Hands: Boots on the ground	**Potential Impact of Outcome of decision on school culture** *Cutting the program entirely may create bad vibes in the community because students have explicitly expressed a desire for it. Not supporting your AP may have adverse impacts as well because being overwhelmed and stressed out can cause lack of leadership in the departments and teams they oversee.*

In each of the examples above, there is a challenge presented that means someone or something will ultimately have to pivot or change which may be to the detriment of the school community. While both examples provide a challenge, the decision should be able to support your AP and have a smaller roll-out of the program. While it may not have been what you envisioned, a smaller start is better than none at all. This means you hire the additional AP to support the community and delegate the responsibilities of the AP you currently have. Another suggestion would be to encourage the AP to find leaders within the departments they supervise as a means of exhibiting distributive leadership and creating a culture where other voices are valued. This imbues trust in your teams and shows that leadership should live in all spaces. When challenges arise, you as a leader have to determine how to offset the impact of financial decisions on the school community. Ultimately, the culturally responsive school leader will try best as possible to ensure that adverse impact on the school community is minimal. There will be cases where this is not possible, but even then, the choice should be contingent upon what causes the least amount of community disruption.

Hiring APs/vice principals is a necessary part of a school community. If you hire the right ones, you are ensuring smooth systems and support for the community. As they are costly, it is important to weigh their financial cost with what they bring. It's important that they too understand and align with your thinking on the impact of financial decisions for the school. Would your AP vote alongside you to cut a bilingual program even if your school population needed it? You want APs who will be equity-minded and help you with your blind spots. The decisions one makes with finances can illuminate a lot about their heart and what they believe is best for children. This starts well before they enter your building, and this is important to reflect on in your hiring practices. Here are some questions to ask during your hiring process that will allow you to assess where one's core values lie aligned with budgeting.

1. If you have to decide between cutting an after-school program and cutting a day school program, what information would you use to make your decision?

2. What are your core values and how does that show up in your role as a leader?
3. If you have students who are not being served based on current programming—ENL students, for example—what changes can you make in order to ensure they are getting their services?
4. You have to decide between cutting a program for vulnerable students or excessing a teacher. Take me through your thought process as you prepare to make a decision.

While some people are interview masters, the questions above provide a glimpse into a person's mindset related to equity-driven decision-making. I would suggest using your actual school data in the interview and posing a challenge that could actually live in your community. The core value activity in the "Introduction" (Chapter 1) should also be used for hiring inquiries as you want to ensure that values align with what you desire for the community at large. If you have time and space, another culturally responsive move would be to place the budgetary decision at the feet of the community to decide. This makes it truly one that is collaborative. The downside of that, using the AP-versus-filmmaking program example, is that others in the community may not always see the value in things the way you do. For some, another AP means an exorbitant cost at the expense of a student program. In this case, refer to the core values and what the impact on the "streets" will be and be transparent about the reason for the need.

Does Your Budget Reflect What You Value?

School budgeting will always be a precarious challenge as it is contingent upon the school year, the number of students in your building, and the needs of the community. You should always make your decisions based on taking all those impacted into account but must primarily be driven by your core values. In the scenarios presented above, there are casualties and unpleasantries that will unfortunately come as you have to make difficult decisions. If your heart is in the right place, if you know who you are as a leader, and if you are able to consult community stakeholders you trust, then you are being a culturally responsive leader in your decision-making, and the chips will fall where they may. The most important thing that can be done when making monetary decisions that will have a resounding impact is to share, share, share as much information as possible with the community. Oftentimes, resentment and negative waves of school culture come from the streets seeing the impacts of decisions being made without having the rationale behind it. While you should not share things that are private challenges only the administrators should know about—an example being you have to follow a directive you have no control over[1]—you as the school leader should share as much as possible about the situation as this will breed trust and empathy for whatever decision was made and will also offer a lens into the school leader's role as a manager who sometimes has to do things they don't like. This picture not only illuminates the humility of your leadership but elicits an element of trust from staff. If they know that there are only two options and that you are deeply thinking through the impact, assumptions about your decision are left to the wayside. Can you endear support or guidance for every decision regarding budget? Of course not. Consulting for every decision means there wouldn't be enough time to make one. What you want, though, is for the streets to see that you are thoughtful and purposeful about the impact of your decisions on the community. It's money in the bank!

Saying the Quiet Part Out Loud: Race and Experience Matter

While I will almost certainly receive dissent and backlash for this, I want to explain why race and experience matter in leadership and within the school community. Let's first address all of the foolishness that will come as some read this subtitle. No, you should not hire someone based solely on race. No, you should not hire someone over someone with similar experience based on race. No, race is not a signifier of academic competence or socio-emotional ability when working with children of color. No, people of similar racial identities are not always aligned in thinking and belief systems. One of my worst educational experiences was in elementary school. Mrs. Muhammad always saw me as a challenge to her authority because I asked too many questions and finished my work quickly while asking for more. I was always in trouble and could do nothing right. One of my most positive memorable experiences was also in elementary school. Ms. Utsey, a statuesque Afro-centric Black woman with the spirit of a warm demander, showed me that I mattered even though I came in third place in the citywide storytelling contest. Both of these women were Black and were part of different educational experiences in my youth. I share this experience to say that there can be differences in experience based on the race of the educator and that having someone the same race as a child is not a predictor of the relationship or outcomes. Here's what else I know to be true. I am a Black woman with locks and never spoke of my race to my students. Yet almost every student I've taught was excited to have me, and when I asked why, they always organically mentioned my race and affect. "I didn't have too many Black teachers, I like the vibe, class is fun." These comments always made me think about my own experience and the similarities. I had three Black teachers total up until college, where I was able to be selective and intentional about the courses I selected. I didn't select based on race, obviously—that's not even an option—but I did select based on the course objectives and content. It just so happened the courses I took were taught by Black educators from across the diaspora or those who were not Black but taught courses that deeply spoke to my values and inquiries. Race matters because it is important for young people to see educators who look like them share an affinity for all they bring and what they learn. This experience can prove powerful, especially when you are able to share commonalities. Sitting in my graduate course with Dr. Wayne Moreland and being enamored with his dissection of James Baldwin lit my soul on fire. He was the most brilliant, Black, laid-back academic I'd ever met and showed me that not all academics were nerdy or pretentious. You could be brilliant and chill at the same time. I wanted my students to see those connections as well. One of my students was excited that I had locks as she was starting hers and wanted to know how to take care of them. This connection lasted beyond when she left my class, and she wrote about it before she graduated. Being in a leadership role now, I have students who come to me excited because they've "never had an AP like me". I say all this to say students strive for a connection and these are sometimes easier when student race, ethnicities, and identities are represented in the community. Having a dope heart and mind are also a blessing and this too creates a safe space for students to thrive. In college, one of my favorite professors introduced me to *Native Son* by Richard Wright. I'd never had such rigorous discourse and such a deep discussion about race and its impact on Black adolescents. This woman was for sure at least 60 and White. She was brilliant and to this day I realize she possessed a heart and mindset that allowed me a space to ask challenging questions because her own experiences and open-mindedness shined through in her teaching. She was the epitome of experience and exposure being precursors to positive relationships. She did not look like me, and she did not have to. She *saw me* and *spoke to me*, even if she didn't know it. Look at your community and ask, "Are all my students/ identities represented on the team or on staff? Do they have someone to go to as a safe space?" It is important to hire based on the identities represented in your building as well as dope hearts and minds aligned with that of the community and student needs and interests. Overall, the connections are what matters and this is always to the benefit of the community.

"What ya pockets looking like?"
Application and Materials

What Ya Pockets Lookin' Like?
Budgeting

Entering	Emerging	Applying	Deepening
I make budgetary decisions based on enrollment numbers. I make decisions in isolation as I know what's best and have all the context.	I try to think of what I want the community should feel like when making budgetary decisions. I inform my administrative team of my decisions to obtain feedback after the fact.	I reflect on my core values in addition to the needs of my school community when making budgetary decisions. I make decisions in consultation with my administrative team/cabinet.	Through my core values and the needs of my community, I make decisions thinking of least amount of negative impact. I consult stakeholders and engage them in the decision-making where possible.

Activity

For the Love of Money!

Use the criteria below to determine what hiring/budgeting needs to happen for your community. Using the data below, write down your ***ideal hiring scenario*** absent of budget. Don't focus so much on the number of teachers needed, just the areas you'd like to see supported.

School Profile

1. High school for students in engineering. Enrollment: 890.
2. 20% of population are ENL students.
3. 25% of students have individualized education plans (IEPs) that designate them as being in need of special education services.
4. A survey showed that students have an interest in sports programs as well as social media content creation and robotics programs.
5. 1 out of 5 students is designated housing-insecure.
6. All students in the school are eligible for Advanced Placement courses in science and math.
7. You need teachers to cover all content areas as normal: math, science, English, gym, and history.
8. You currently have two assistant/vice principals who cover multiple subjects each.

Scenario-Based Practice:

Joke's on you!

You've outlined the ideal hiring plan in the activity above. Good for you!

Now for the fun part:
Your imaginary budget has just been cut in half. From the information provided above and the decisions you've made about hiring, who or what is on the chopping block?

Keep in mind your core values and strive for the greatest amount of positive impact and the least amount of adverse impact.

We Like Big Books and I Cannot Lie
Reads to get you thinking

Note

1 The school leader should not ever create or cause factions in their community. Saying something is being "forced" or that you do not agree with it implies that staff do not have to support it. This is a dangerous path that undermines what you ultimately need done, which is compliance and belief in the initiative. Sometimes, you have to take one for the team and grit your teeth, and that's real.

References

Chatterjee, R. (2024, July). *When little kids don't have stable housing, it can affect their health later.* NPR. https://www.npr.org/sections/shots-health-news/2024/07/01/nx-s1-5019537/housing-insecurity-childhood-health-depression-anxiety

Godoy, M. (2023, October 26). *Millions of American families struggle to get food on the table, report finds.* NPR. https://www.npr.org/sections/health-shots/2023/10/26/1208760054/food-insecurity-families-struggle-hunger-poverty

Hahnel, C. (2020, October). *California's education funding crisis explained in 12 charts*. Policy Analysis for California Education. https://edpolicyinca.org/publications/californias-education-funding-crisis-explained-12-charts

Additional Reading

Tatum, B. D. (2017). *"Why are all the black kids sitting together in the cafeteria?": And other conversations about race*. Basic Books.

5

Instructional Core

You Are *What They* Teach!

The School Leader as an Instructional Leader

Now that you've interrogated yourself and values, had some very uncomfortable conversations with staff, cried over difficult budgetary decisions, and tried your absolute best to cultivate a school culture grounded in equity, it's time to focus on what them children are learning! Being a leader means that even if you are not able to be present in classrooms on a consistent basis, you are ultimately responsible for what is taught and how it is taught. Curriculum and instruction impact a school's culture in the same way that dissenting views and misunderstandings between staff do—it throws off the VIBE. In order to ensure that students are obtaining required learning to meet graduation requirements and pass their tests, curriculum and instruction needs to be aligned with state standards and learning goals. If you are ensuring that this is taking place by purchasing the necessary curricula for every content area and meeting with team leaders to reflect on student data a few times a year, you are at minimum doing what is required. To be a culturally responsive leader, though, you need to take it a step further and be an instructional leader who values and supports culturally responsive pedagogy.

Being an "instructional leader" is layered and has multiple meanings depending upon who is asked. It means being able to speak deeply to what is being taught—knowing assessments, standards being addressed, and specific content and ways of engaging learners at all levels. Being an instructional leader also means supporting teachers with how to adapt and modify what students are learning based on your own understanding of the content and materials present. Lastly, being an instructional leader means being able to model or speak to the strongest and most relevant strategies in education for teaching and learning. As the fearless leader of the school building, also in charge of budgeting, attending all of the "extremely necessary" meetings you have, ensuring that teachers and other stakeholders see you as a positive and supportive presence, you have PLENTY of time to be an instructional leader, right? Absolutely wrong. I was taught in my licensing program that I needed to be an instructional leader as I would be responsible for what was taught in classrooms. With this I agree, but this does not look like being in every content meeting and planning alongside teachers. You need to have both a macro and micro view of the learning and experiences of students. I would take it a step further and say that, as a leader, I find that my core values are represented not just in *what* is taught but *how* it is taught. Do I ever have time to be present in classrooms as much as I'd like and attend department meetings? Nope. But this is where culturally responsive leadership comes into play.

Curriculum and Instruction Can Throw Off the V.I.B.E

School culture is impacted by a variety of variables, but one of the most important is what students are learning and how teachers are teaching. As educators and lifelong learners, we are taught that we are the arbitrators of the knowledge aligned with our content areas. For myself as an English teacher, I was an overseer of all things English. It was important for me as a teacher to reflect on this perceived "power" and do the right thing with it. While I could have been a pedantic English teacher and focused on the American English Conventions at all times, I knew two things to be sure. I hated every teacher I came across who refused to let me speak my mind in ways I felt comfortable, and you have to meet young people where they are by validating their authenticity and letting them know they are safe to be themselves as they learn. Did this mean I didn't take the red pen (green in my case) to their essays or that I didn't push them to be critical in their writing and reflections on prose? Nah. What it did mean was that when I asked a student what Paul Laurence Dunbar meant when he said, "We Wear the Mask," and they said "He means we have to front sometimes," I accepted that answer, deeply agreed and knew what they meant. Dunbar spoke of the experiences of Blacks after the Civil War and the fact that outward contentment was more palatable to others than the exhibition of the inward suffering. I pushed for more from this student and then we discussed what the poem means overall as well as how it's connected to our lived experiences. I say this to state that teachers can make or break a student's educational experience and therein lies the danger with curriculum and instruction (Love, 2019).[1] It can be used to enlighten and cultivate, or it can be used as a tool to ostracize and signal to students they do not belong. In my example above, had I been the teacher who told that student, "Use proper English," not only would it have turned them off from sharing but it could also have made them feel like my classroom was not a safe space. Encounters like these are resounding for students and if compounded every day—by different teachers and different classes—the *school*, and not the instruction, becomes the issue. This can inadvertently become attributed to the "culture" of the school. One bad apple can spoil the bunch when it comes to teaching and relationships. What you want to avoid is having what students are lacking in classrooms be an indicator of the overall "VIBE" in your community.

What is a school leader to do in this situation? If you don't know what students are experiencing, there's no way to address the relationships and learning happening in classrooms. You can go about ascertaining what students are experiencing by talking to them. This can be done in a variety of ways such as surveys, talking to teachers and department chairs, classroom walkthroughs, and other informal data—the list goes on. As the leader, you should first set clear expectations around what you want teaching in your school building to look like and then support teachers and stakeholders with seeing this through. This process is challenging and will require buy-in (we will talk about that a little later in depth), but since we can't be in classrooms as much as we like and may not be present consistently in larger meetings, we have to provide our department leaders an administrative team with non-negotiables for curriculum and instruction rooted in our leadership core values and belief system.

Curriculum & Instruction Should Be a VIBE

There are numerous sources that speak to how we can implement culturally responsive practices in education (culturally responsive education [CRE] or culturally responsive-sustaining education [CRSE]). When I was in my teacher education program in the 2010s, there wasn't much of a focus on CRSE as a practice, let alone clear key strategies for implementation. The scholarship was present as there were academics such as Dr. Gloria Ladson Billings who spoke deeply about the need for education being used as a lever to affirm, deepen, and critique the learning of students in schools. However, unless you're a nerd like me, you don't have time to read over scholarly articles or deeply engross yourself in academic reading—you're already reading this!—so here is a layman's view on CRSE.

What Is CRSE or CRE?

CRE and CRSE are both terms derived from Dr. Ladson Billings's work. Culturally responsive pedagogy (CRP) was coined by Billings and stressed the importance of education as a collective and was intended to be a pedagogy of opposition. Culturally relevant pedagogy requires students to "experience academic success, develop/maintain cultural competence, and develop a critical consciousness through which they challenge the status quo of the current social order" (Ladson-Billings, 1995: 160). The acronym CRSE comes from the addition of wanting to continually focus on "sustaining" and "emerging" issues in educational landscapes. She describes each of the tenets in her own words in

"But That's Just Good Teaching! The Case for Culturally Relevant Pedagogy":

On academic success

> students must develop their academic skills. The way those skills are developed may vary, but all students need literacy, numeracy, technological, social, and political skills in order to be active participants in a democracy.
>
> (160)

On cultural competence

> Culturally relevant teachers utilize students' culture as a vehicle for learning...another way teachers can support cultural competence is by including parents in the classroom...students can learn from one another's parents and affirm cultural knowledge". A third example of maintaining cultural competence is by encouraging students to use their home language while they acquired the secondary discourse of 'standard' English.
>
> (160)

On critical consciousness

> Culturally relevant teaching does not imply that it is enough for students to choose academic excellence and remain culturally grounded if those skills and abilities represent only an individual achievement...Students must develop a broader sociopolitical consciousness that allows them to critique the cultural norms, values, mores and institutions that produce and maintain social inequities. If school is about preparing students for active citizenship, what better citizenship tool than the ability to critically analyze society?
>
> (161)

These tenets sound simple enough. We as educators should want all of our students to feel at home in their classrooms, be affirmed by their interactions and engagements with their teachers and peers, and work toward being citizens who are able to think deeply and critically about injustices in their world. The hope is that students will use critique as an entry point to examine their views and as a lever for change. These three tenets are an oversimplification of CRP, but each iteration of CRSE or CRE is derived from this framework. The challenge lies in the fact that there are certain skills and strategies you can't teach teachers. These are the teachers who do lots of invisible work in their classrooms to build those connections and relationships that translate so seamlessly into effective pedagogy. There are just some teachers who possess a strong sense of their core values and have a deep understanding of their culture or the cultures of others, and this oozes in their instructional practices and approaches. There will be challenges when trying to evaluate if teachers possess an intrinsic value system that is CRSE-aligned. Unfortunately, no amount of training, coaching, or workshops can make someone value another person's cultural contributions or see their worth in academic spaces. This work is deeply internal and requires a willingness both within and outside of academic spaces. While everyone can teach skills and standards, the *way* they are taught is more important than the educator's resume and qualifications. The message may seem discouraging as I am definitely saying there is "person work" that goes into being a culturally conscious educator. So what is a school leader to do when staff don't already possess this lens? My plea is that you create an instructional expectation that is strong and rooted in your core values and Dr. Billings's work. The hope is that those who have not done the internal work or are unwilling to do so won't be able to fit into the culture and will eventually unsubscribe by seeing themselves out! Educators who are not amenable to what you as the school leader desire with instruction so long as it's in the best interest of young people need a clear system for accountability, conversations, and expectations.

The *V.I.B.E. [curriculum & instruction edition]* model is a great way to start the conversation.

Before assessing the VIBE around curriculum and instruction, you should determine what you value and how that shows up, or does not show up, in your view on teaching and learning. Here's an inquiry cycle to work through before we get into this work!

TABLE 5.1 Leadership Curriculum Value Alignment

1. What are you core values when it comes to teaching and learning?
2. What do you want students to experience in their academic spaces?
3. What elements of citizenship do you value and want to impart?
4. Is the current curriculum representative of the school community?

VIBE: Curriculum & Instruction Edition

In Chapter 3, I provide a VIBE model for assessing school culture, and this acronym provides a means of interrogating the community to better understand its needs and culture. As a recap, a "VIBE" is a noun used in an informal manner. It is defined as "a person's emotional state or the atmosphere of a place as communicated to and felt by others" (Cambridge Dictionary, 2024). A VIBE can be felt and does not require a verbal declaration of it in order for it to be felt and understood. A person can be "bad vibes" through their actions, "energy" being emitted into a space, or simply by how they present themselves around others. In the interim, a person can experience bad vibes based on how they are impacted by others in a specific space or within their presence. A building or classroom can also be bad vibes based on what is happening or what is *not* happening. "Good vibes" also exist and are ever present in spaces where one feels joy and safety. We all have unspoken expectations around how we want to be received and what various spaces should *feel* like. The classroom should never be "bad vibes" but it can be if the instruction or teacher is!

Let's test your ability to read the vibe before the formula:

TABLE 5.2 Scenarios 1 and 2: Assess the VIBE

Scenario 1: Assess the VIBE	*Scenario 2: Assess the VIBE*
You walk into an ICT (integrated co-teaching) classroom, and there is music playing on the smartboard. Students are working in pairs, and there is one teacher sitting with a group of five. The other teacher is circulating to support other pairs or teams. As the bell rings, students don't immediately get up to leave but instead walk out while singing the song playing to one another. The teacher walks to the door to say bye to students as they leave.	You walk into a classroom, and students are sitting in rows. They are each working on a task, and this is clear because instructions are on the board. The board says students are to be QUIET while working. You ask the teacher if students are taking a test, and they say, "No, it's today's lesson, but I don't want them having the chance to get out of control".

Based on the examples above, which classroom would you desire to be part of? I would argue that each example shows what the educator in those spaces values. In scenario 1, students are working and being supported while listening to music they appreciate. This teacher values student discourse and creating a VIBE that is conducive to learning but also makes students feel comfortable. Scenario 2 shows that the teacher values compliance and their own idea of "safety" as they require students to engage in the learning in a way that makes them as the educator feel comfortable. Whereas scenario 2 may demonstrate that the teacher struggles with management and therefore chooses active and visible compliance over student discourse, scenario 1 shows that systems and structures can be implemented where learning can happen *and* students feel safe and comfortable. I hear some of you readers already, "What does this have to do with curriculum and instruction?" Young people and people in general don't learn in environments where they feel unsafe or devalued. Before you jump into the technical curriculum fixes, you better make damn sure the environment and interactions are positive and conducive to the students' feeling like they belong and are valued.

Now that you've focused on the physical VIBE, let's get into this curriculum work! In full transparency, this VIBE curriculum model is driven by my own core values in alignment with culturally responsive practices. Using this as a lever for implementation of and modification of the curriculum being taught is a means of ensuring that all students and experiences are being centered within their learning. We will unpack the potential off-ramps, as I'm sure they will arise, but it's important to reflect first and have a deep understanding of this model in practice.

The *VIBE [curriculum and instruction edition]* requires us to ask "What's the VIBE?" in our buildings aligned with curriculum

TABLE 5.3 What's the V.I.B.E?: Curriculum and Instruction Edition

- *V (voices and visibility)*
- *I (interrogation and inquiry)*
- *B (backwards design)*
- *E (extensions and evaluations)*

and instruction. In this case, the model can be used to evaluate a curriculum before it is brought into a community. It can also be used to interrogate a lesson or an educator's practice as they are instructing. Each of the letters plays a pertinent role in the way students receive and participate in their learning experience. It also pushes educators to think deeply about what they are teaching by weaving culturally responsive tenets into the learning and landscape. As the school leader, you should be encouraging and supporting staff with the use of the VIBE model within their curriculum and instruction. You can also use this model yourself as you enter classrooms, engage in curriculum audits and evaluations, and talk to teachers about their student needs.

V [Voices and Visibility]

Every curriculum is representative of culture. The question is whose culture is dominant and if there are stories about other cultures, what lens are they being taught from? One way to ensure that good vibes are present in practice is to include voices of various groups as well as different points of views on their experiences. It is important to assess what narratives are visible or invisible within the instruction and make the necessary modifications to address gaps or omissions. The purpose of this is to ensure that students are being exposed to all parts of a narrative, even ones that may be deemed harmful (more on that in the "I" section), as a means of reflecting on the experiences of people who share their culture in addition to the experiences of others. This aligns with Dr. Billings's tenets of cultural competence and critical consciousness as students will be asked to evaluate not just different cultures but also the experiences and norms that may be harmful or an affront to equity for all.

I [Interrogation and Inquiry]

Critical thinking is a lifelong skill. We should interrogate and inquire about narratives within curriculum and instruction as pre-scripted curriculum is written by teams and groups of people at large education companies. While they are well intended and have more recently included various voices and narratives as part of their curricula, curriculum writers are human beings and educators just like us. We all have different lenses and experiences that drive what we believe to be critical instructional practice. Additionally, curriculum companies provide materials to a widely encompassing base. Does the lesson hit for kids in New York City as it does for kids in South Dakota? Only teachers know the students sitting in front of them and the stories they hold. It is important for teachers to interrogate EVERYTHING in a lesson or curriculum from the essential questions to the student tasks and texts as a means of intellectually reaching the kids in front of them. Examples of interrogation or inquiry of a lesson would be questions like

- How does this (essential question) connect to the lived experiences of my students?
- What are the unintended consequences of teaching this lesson exclusively in the way it was written?
- What precontext do my students need to be successful in reaching this learning target?
- Is there a historical context necessary to understand the larger social issues at play?

Deeper questions include

- Am I providing opportunities for students to feel affirmed in their culture or learn about the cultures of others?
- Are there harmful narratives that need to be unpacked or explored with students and addressed as part of this learning?
- Is there a dominant conversation regarding this topic or lens? Am I addressing all sides?

It is important to address even narratives that may seem harmful as they are often reflections of time periods and ideologies that permeate the fabric of society. The only way to learn from and not give a home to hateful, racist, homophobic, ableist, or sexist rhetoric is to allow students a space to speak about and learn about them. Students should also learn about the structures and systems that allow inequitable systems to thrive. This too aligns with Dr. Billings's premise of cultural competence and critical consciousness. An example of this interrogation/inquiry would be the language used in *Native Son* by Richard Wright or *To Kill a Mockingbird* by Harper Lee. Both of these texts use derogatory terms to refer to African Americans due to the time period they were written in. We shouldn't ban books or ideas that make us uncomfortable as they are snapshots in time, reflections of unfortunate moments in history. We should contextualize them and the challenges they present today but acknowledge the history they are tethered to. This is the true measure of providing a space for critical thinking. Thinking critically means hearing all sides of an argument and, given your value system, drawing your own conclusion while deciding what's best for your heart and the heart of others. If no other space can support this in a young person's life, the classroom must. If young people are agreeing with everything they're exposed to, I can almost guarantee the VIBE is wack.

B [Backwards Design]

This letter is a little boring if I do say so myself but is very necessary. The Understanding by Design Model (Wiggins and McTighe, 2005) asks educators to plan their lessons and learning with the end assessment in mind. This is a culturally responsive practice only if the end assessment is being interrogated to determine if it allows for critical thinking and multi-layered perspectives as part of the summative assessment. Sure, you can have students write an essay about Christopher Columbus and his accomplishments as part of their final task on the colonization of the Americas, but if students are not also asked about Columbus's perception as one who participated in the genocide of Native Americans, is the task culturally responsive and promoting critical thinking? I would argue it is not. Backwards design is an integral part of creating/supporting a culturally responsive curriculum as teachers will need to first determine if the ends justify the asks within their instruction. This level of engagement and planning requires one to be proactive as opposed to responsive in their planning for a student's instructional needs. This also allows for the integration of learning scaffolds and supports for students who may struggle with the standards and skills that are part of the task. Modification for access and opportunity are just as important as pushes for deep intellectual engagement. If you have special education students or students in need of varied access points, how are you supporting them with this? Sure, rich culturally responsive questions about the world and real-world application are great, but if we are not seeing the personhood of our students through the lens of their needs, what is it all for? You don't need a "special population" to center student needs. Every child has learning needs and it's up to us to find out what works best. This is also culturally responsive and aligns with Dr. Billings's pillar of academic success!

An example of this is in Table 5.4.

TABLE 5.4 Backwards Design Evaluation

Backwards Design CRSE evaluation:

Task: Students will write an essay about Josef K, the protagonist in Franz Kafka's *The Trial* (…)* and his ability to persevere even in the face of challenges.

Questions to ask: What were the challenges he faced? Do any of these speak to larger social issues that students can address? Is there a power struggle? Does he truly persevere or does he concede in the face of challenges?

> * *The Trial* is a wonderful book to discuss issues of oppression from systems and the ways individualism is futile in the face of larger social structures.

In the example, one must first know of the challenges presented to the protagonist. Josef is arrested at the onset of the text without being told why. He spends the entire text attempting to understand his incarceration and the reasoning behind it but to no avail. The reader also does not know. He is continually met with bureaucracy, bereft of clarity, and is simply told to talk to one person after another. Ultimately, he succumbs to his arrest and is victim to a system that is oppressive and sees him as an object not worthy of saving. Planning with this end task in mind means knowing that the text is centered on corruption and oppression and that the question about his "perseverance" needs to address the fact that he was oppressed. Despite what I would refer to as his "insistence" versus perseverance, in order for the end task to be culturally responsive students need to be taught explicitly about the criminal justice system and its functioning as a panopticon for the protagonist. They should also explore what the text implies about the subordinate and powerless role of citizens when faced with larger social institutions. Without reviewing the end task and knowing the contents of the text, the learning has the potential to lack culturally responsive elements such as aligning with societal challenges and being a source for student evaluation of systems and structures.

E [Extensions]

When I as an educator hear the term "extensions" in alignment with curriculum and instruction, I automatically think about how I am providing additional material that is more challenging or literally "extends" the learning. This letter asks us to do just that but adds another layer. The "E" in the VIBE model asks teachers to provide students with the opportunity to extend their thinking by positing new challenges, engaging in research about the topic to uncover new things, and adding their own layer of need to the lesson. Examples of this would be the teacher providing a survey that asks students what they know about the topic being discussed and what they would like to know more about. It would also be students crafting a response to a present challenge in society or within the lesson that would be a change in a particular law, state mandate, and so on. In the V.I.B.E. model, the goals of the extension are student engagement and citizenship. That is, how can we provide an opportunity in our instruction for students to craft a world they want to live in or make sense of. Billings also advocated for the inclusion of the family in the learning of students (161). This would also serve as a culturally responsive extension as it would allow for learning about, through actual stories, the histories and viewpoints of other cultures.

Let's practice applying the VIBE curriculum model!
Looking at the sample unit plan overview, how we can use the VIBE model to assess for cultural responsiveness.

TABLE 5.5 Native Son Unit Plan Overview

Unit Plan: 8th-grade English
Text: *Native Son* by Richard Wright
Final Task Assessment: Is Bigger Thomas a victim or villain? Prepare a defense for him on trial OR a case for prosecution using evidence from the text and your research.

Overarching Essential Question and Weekly Research Focus:
Free will: Do we as humans all act on "free will" or are there factors that impact the decisions we choose to make?

Free-will: Does it exist? What does this look like in the face of adversity? Should other factors be considered?
Environment: Are we "products of our environment?" Are there instances where our "environment" can positively/negatively impact our decisions?
Family/Financial Status: Does our upbringing and family make-up impact the decisions we make as an adolescent?
Race/Gender/Sexual Orientation: Do we believe that any of these will present challenges in the face of decisions or will impact decisions we choose to make? Why? How?
Systems and Structures: In the face of adverse decisions, are outcomes always the same for those with different challenges above?

V: Are there varied voices and experiences?

I: Are there opportunities for inquiry and interrogation of systems and structures or experiences?

B: If planning with the assessment in mind, is there an opportunity for critical thinking aligned with the weekly foci and essential question?

E: Can students create civic-oriented solutions to the challenges presented in each week or extend their learning about the topics through research on their own and apply it to a larger social context?

Support the Ask (Space and Grace)

You are asking a lot of educators with the inclusion of the VIBE model or use of this lens. Educators are counselors, nurses, peer mediators, snack connoisseurs, and much more throughout their day. To support implementation of the model, your program for the day has to provide space for teachers to meet and align their thinking for what they will teach. While a leader can say, "The program allows for two preparation periods per day, they can meet then!," the culturally responsive leader would be intentional about creating strategic and purposeful periods for collaboration as both a grade and department. There's no better teacher than collaboration and inquiry alongside people who have the same challenges as you. In this case, the challenge is teaching in a manner that is culturally responsive. If you don't allocate and support intentional collaborative time, the message received will be that the implementation of culturally responsive tenets is optional. In order for good vibes to thrive in the curriculum, you as the leader have to cultivate it with purposeful programmatic alignment. Taking it a step further, the program should also provide time for teachers to interrogate their belief systems and mindsets around race, their own experiences as students, special student populations, and more. The VIBE model can be taught, but if your head and heart are not in the right place, it is all for naught. As a leader, ask yourself, what do educators in my building believe about children? Children of color? The community we serve? Our student demographic? I'd also suggest you provide space for educators in your community to grapple with these questions themselves alongside colleagues as a form of internal and external reflection.

You plan for "people work" in your structured use of time. Through the use of data from the school aligned with student demographic and experiences with their learning both inside and outside of the community, you should program for purposeful discussions and learning for your community—not just on culturally responsive education and its tenets but also about the community at large. Here's an example:

TABLE 5.6 Equity-Driven Professional Learning

Investing in "People Work": Equity-Driven Professional Learning
You lead a staff meeting to go over the changing demographics of your community. While the population used to be predominantly Asian, it is shifting to be more African-American and Albanian. You lead a staff professional learning to go over the shift and interrogate what we think we know about these communities. You also share the median family income and census data. You encourage staff to think about how they can support both of these communities and evaluate what their mental models are about them. You also survey parents and families about their needs and interests.

In the example above, you are naming a shift in the demographics of the community. This should be used to provide a space to evaluate their mental models about these groups and what they perceive their needs to be. It will also be important to go over demographics as it allows for them to have an understanding of the community they serve without making assumptions. This work will ask staff to reflect on their core values aligned with their teaching and the needs of students. This reflective work should be done often and with purpose aligned with the community and outcomes for students. The purpose? Determining the needs of those you serve. If there is a need for your students to see more narratives about the immigrant experience, the focus should be what the tales of the students are and how to integrate them into the overall learning. This requires also listening to the voices of students and families as to not make assumptions and to truly meet their needs.

Roadblocks and Your Role as Leader

Start with Your Leadership Teams

It is important to set the expectation for your community that you are an instructional leader—not in the sense that you will be in classrooms every day or will help to write and modify curriculum but in the sense that what is taught is a reflection of your beliefs around pedagogy and the student experience. It should be made clear that instructional expectations are part of your larger vision and belief system as a school leader, all of which are driven by your core values. If you are a leader who believes in culturally responsive instruction and its tenets, the VIBE model allows you to have a clear reference point for stakeholders to understand your lens on instruction and apply it across various departments. This is where buy-in, stakeholder voice, the administrative team, and your instructional leads come into play. Since you can't be in all spaces, it is important to have allies that will support and integrate the model into all possible areas. When administrators are doing evaluations and instructional rounds, they should reference the model. When coaches and instructional leads are engaging in rounds or supporting teachers, they should utilize the model. When departments are meeting to plan lessons and evaluate assessments, the model should be present. When you are meeting with parents and families, they should know what instructional lens you value and should be able to ask questions about the model. All of this will ensure that when you are running around doing big boss things, your core values and the VIBE model are able to live within the fabric of the school culture.

Structures Are Not Enough: Invest in the "Heart" Work

V.I.B.E is a cute little acronym that is great and serves as a point of reference for your culturally responsive values. However, we all know that implementing a structure and then saying "I expect to see this everywhere" is not a predictor of said structure's success. Culturally responsive practices require a practitioner/educator to believe fundamentally in its basic premise: students come into school buildings with histories and stories that deserve to be heard and valued as part of their learning. Anyone who doesn't believe this wouldn't be an educator, right? Wrong. There are people who are in education and are wildly unaware of their biases as we are all amalgamations of our own lived experiences. There doesn't have to be malicious intent for someone to unconsciously invalidate the experience of another. The problem arises in the community if a person is made aware they possess a harmful ideology and refuse to be reflective and make change. As a leader, you oftentimes hire based on a dire need or a resume that seems to align with your core values. It is important at all stages—and for all teachers regardless of year or content area—to reflect on their own lived experiences, how those experiences have shaped them as a person, and how that impacts their teaching philosophy daily. Through this self-interrogation, there should also be work that is intentionally focused on one's biases, narratives they've been taught about others, and ways to disrupt and push back against them for the sake of the young people they encounter each day. Just as important is supporting, highlighting, and celebrating teachers who are engaging in the work as they are also allies who will allow your message and values to permeate not just the classroom but also teacher teams and informal conversations with colleagues. This all impacts school culture. There will be some people who present as potential challengers due to their apprehension. This is when using the "I" inquiry portion of the V.I.B.E. school culture model (Chapter 3) will be important because there is a grave difference between unwillingness and inability due to personal discomfort. Discomfort can be worked through if the root cause is addressed. Does the teacher not have shared experiences that allow for a diverse or culturally responsive lens? Are they willing but don't know how? These are challenges you can support. The affect that threatens the VIBE is the unknowing and unwilling. An educator who does not know their blind spots but is also dogmatic in their approach will be harder to support. Sometimes, you have to support someone into an environment that is more their speed—even if it's not yours. One of the most profound questions I've heard asked of those who present challenges due to their unwillingness is "What's standing in your way?" This question moved me because it seeks to get deep at the core of a person's feelings and beliefs, all while seeking to support or surface their own reluctance. Holding a mirror up and having to look in it to own and name your stuff can be life-changing.

TABLE 5.7 Brief CRSE Inquiry Cycle

→ What do you know or what is your belief about culturally responsive education?
→ Where did you grow up? What was the demographic?
→ What kinds of schools did you attend and how does that impact your teaching experience/ethos?
→ Are there any topics that make you uncomfortable to teach? Why?
→ How do you feel about banning books or concepts?

State/Region/Jurisdictional Challenges

When I first started as a teacher, I had the liberty of writing the curriculum I wanted to teach. The first book I taught was Richard Wright's *Native Son* as I was so enamored with the experience of Bigger Thomas as well as the questions created by his tale about society and its imbalance for young Black males. I also loved the fact that I was able to include historical context—serving as a humanities-oriented unit—as the text was set in 1930s segregated

South Side of Chicago. Redlining and housing laws during that time allowed for rich discourse and a look at US history that otherwise would not be discussed in classrooms. There are many places where culturally responsive tenets—specifically, critical thinking and socio-political consciousness—are discouraged, and in some places they are downright illegal. This may seem like an off-ramp or a reason for choosing to not engage in these practices. If you are using this as a reason to not engage in the work, I push you to ask yourself why. My suggestion in the face of outright objection to culturally responsive practices is to break down the model and reduce them to what each letter represents. The ideas of critical thinking, participation in citizenship, and discussing various viewpoints are things everyone should want for their children. If there is opposition to any of these, the issue is larger than what students are learning in classrooms and wherever you are is just "bad vibes". There is always a justification and defense for thinking critically. That is, of course, unless you are intentionally trying to shape the narrative. That never happens in education, right? I would encourage you as a leader to lean into the examination and critique of curriculum through the use of VIBE as you are not asking for anyone to teach things that are untrue. In fact, you are doing just the opposite. You desire to open a door for young people who will become citizens who don't regurgitate popular media but instead are able to listen to, interpret, and dissect arguments on their own. They then use this and their own belief systems to form opinions. There have to be non-negotiables in your core values and leadership. CRP and positive relationships are two of mine.

Get into It: Other Challenges

Parents are a large part of ensuring that the curriculum has support within a community. It is my belief that they are not always included. While they do not always know what's being taught lesson-to-lesson, they should have a clear system for exposure, inquiry, and feedback as part of the curriculum. Most pushback comes from lack of exposure or understanding. It can also come from false narratives around what students learn or do not learn. Lots of technical terms are being irresponsibly thrown around the current educational landscape and are being wildly conflated with no understanding—for example, culturally responsive education versus critical race theory. Asking parents to learn about their child's learning and what the school values is an important part of implementation. The more you communicate and are transparent, you can answer questions to quell anxiety. While there will be some whose value system poses a challenge to what is taught, at least you were transparent and allowed families to choose their inclusion. This builds trust in the community as well. The danger of not communicating is misinformation.

One day during my third year of teaching, I was out sick and my principal called to ask about a lesson I taught. He'd received a call from a parent who said I was teaching about Black Lives Matter, and they threatened to go to the news. I did teach about Black Lives Matter. What the parent did not know was that I also taught about Blue Lives Matter and All Lives Matter as part of my grade's social justice unit. I sent over the unit plan to my principal as well as the lessons and articles used all to show that I was not "indoctrinating" anyone's child. I was posing different viewpoints and perspectives aligned with an issue that was a relevant topic at the time. Did I tell students to choose a movement? Not at all. What I did do was show all sides of an argument and pose critical thinking questions for them to decide for themselves. Luckily for me, this lens kept me out of trouble, but ultimately it was the parent's lack of knowledge about what was being taught that caused the anxiety and disruption. In the face of challenges aligned with the VIBE [curriculum & instruction model], it is important to provide space and grace for learning for all members of the community. If students are learning about oppression and inequitable systems, shouldn't staff members and families too? Do not waver even in the face of challenges, as our babies deserve to learn and flourish as active participants in their experiences. James Baldwin stated, "The purpose of education is to create in a person the ability to look at the world for himself, to make his own decisions" (Baldwin, 2008). Without administrative support for culturally responsive curriculum and instruction, the world Baldwin spoke of will elude us all.

"You Are What they Teach"
Application and Materials

Is it a VIBE?			
Curriculum and Instruction Edition			
Entering	Emerging	Applying	Deepening
It's impossible to be an instructional leader as I oversee the school building and all its areas. Teachers are the arbitrators of knowledge, and I allow them to lead this conversation.	The region or district mandates my curricular choices, and I do not have a choice. I do not require modification or adaptation as I see it as a deviation from the curriculum. I consult my administrative team about the curriculum and the process for implementation and feedback.	I evaluate all choices of curriculum presented alongside my department leads and administrative team. We then discuss what's best based on the community needs. I set my core values and school values at the forefront of the inquiry process.	I share my core values with stakeholders and name CRSE as a requirement. We together discuss the options available and determine what best meets the needs of the community. We have SHARED values that are represented in the curriculum/modification process.

Activity

MODEL the VIBE

We were all teachers once!

Even though we are in leadership positions, we are still learners. Choose a content area and a lesson to apply the VIBE model. As you do this, think of how you would want the lesson taught or modified to include *Voice, Interrogation, Backwards Design,* and *Extensions*

Think: Are there omissions that need to be added? Are there "good vibes" that can be leveraged and expanded upon? Are there narratives that are untold? Misrepresentations that need to be checked? What staff work needs to be done to lay the foundation? Which teams are ready for this? Which teams aren't?

Scenario-Based Practice:

How do you show up in the face of pushback?

Use the example below to plan a response to a teacher whose lens does not align with culturally responsive tenets. Think: How would you respond? What support will they need? How do you go about attempting to shift their mindset?

You've just gone into a math classroom where they are teaching about the COVID-19 pandemic. The teacher is using statistics to discuss the rates of those impacted in different parts of the world. While the lesson is rigorous and aligned with standards, race is not present in the breakdown and neither is the disproportionality of those impacted in different areas.

How do you engage this teacher in discussing the ways COVID disproportionately impacted Black/Brown and minority communities? How do you support them with creating a space for discourse? How do you get them to see the value and importance of this additional lens?

#CRSEReads
Notable Literature for the people

Note

1 Love (2019) has a chapter on Educational Survival that speaks to this idea deeply. See that book for a more in-depth discussion on "spirit murdering" in education and its impact on children of color.

Bibliography

Baldwin, J. (2008). A talk to teachers. *Teachers College Record: The Voice of Scholarship in Education, 110*(14), 17–20. https://doi.org/10.1177/016146810811001405

Cambridge Dictionary. (2024, June 12). *vibe*. @CambridgeWords. https://dictionary.cambridge.org/us/dictionary/english/vibe#google_vignette

Kafka, F. (2009). *The Trial*. Turtleback Books. (Original work published 1925.)

Ladson-Billings, G. (1995). But that's just good teaching! The case for culturally relevant pedagogy. *Theory into Practice, 34*(3), 159–165. https://doi.org/10.1080/00405849509543675

Love, B. (2019). *We want to do more than survive: Abolitionist teaching and the pursuit of educational freedom*. Beacon.

Wiggins, G., & McTighe, J. (2005). *Understanding by design* (2nd ed.). Association for Supervision and Curriculum Development.

Additional Reading

Haberman, M. (2010). The pedagogy of poverty versus good teaching. *Phi Delta Kappan, 92*(2), 81–87. https://doi.org/10.1177/003172171009200223

6

Capacity Building

That's Your People?

In all spaces, your appointments are a reflection of your belief systems. When you are not around, the people you've placed in leadership positions or shown support and trust for are being closely critiqued just as much as you are. This means you better make some real hard decisions when it comes to the people you place in positions of perceived power and ensure that they match your vibe when it comes to how you lead. Your leadership team should not be carbon copies of your leadership style, as different community members should have different entry points if there is a need. If you're a recluse with great ideas but need support with people skills, there should be people on your team who are warm extroverts that people can trust. Your team should be able to talk that talk the way you do when it comes to school culture, shared values, and belief systems but should also be able to have challenging conversations with you and others when there's a need. An example of this would be if you are making a decision that has the potential to have adverse impacts you don't foresee. Your team leads should be able to talk to you openly and help you make the right decision. The hard part? Selecting leaders. The even more challenging part? *Inheriting* leadership.

A Leader in Title or in Movements?

I was and still am a dope teacher. This I knew without question and there was no contest. I never had a desire to be a school leader because I felt a great amount of unwillingness when it came to leading or supervising adults. I found solace in my ability to say "that's crazy" and bear no responsibility on outcomes for challenges. It was and still is an area where I do not always feel confident in my abilities. I am plagued by imposter syndrome[1] daily and often feel like someone else may be better qualified. Young people and the classroom were my safe spaces. Kids kept it real and were easy to talk to, and my strategies almost always worked. It didn't hurt that they threw me parties and still came back to visit after they graduated. To them, I made a difference. It was visible every day. I went and obtained my leadership license at the behest of my former principal and mentor, who is an absolute monster. He's intimidating because he's so damn smart you have to come correct. He is now a superintendent and could easily lead at the state level. Being a professional student with nothing else to do, I figured, why not go back to school? It's another degree. COVID unexpectedly unleashed its head during this time, but what I learned from my program was that I did value community and relationships. I had the honor of learning from and alongside some of the dopest educators across the Bronx. My summer spent with them taught me that dissent is not always problematic, community means love and grace, and humility can come in the form of learning new things about yourself and how you impact others. I didn't go into the program as a leader. But because of my Bronx cohort members and our leader, I had the best examples of what leadership looked like. I am also eternally grateful to all the administrators and leaders I work alongside daily. Every last person possesses a lens centered on what's best for young people, and they all have attributes that make me aspire to be like them one day.

During Covid, my Assistant Principal—whom we will refer to as "Kane"—became Principal, and the subtle nudging began after I graduated from my program. He was a visionary and was always supportive of my pedagogy and culturally responsive practices when I was a teacher. As I now had a leadership license, he had plans. I was already a coach and support for my department. I worked with the district, showcased for other schools, and had experience with some administratively adjacent tasks, so "leadership" wasn't new. What these things affirmed for me, though, was that I wanted no parts of the real thing. I can vividly remember a conversation Principal Kane had with me about leadership. I huffed and moaned and gave him all of my grievances about why it didn't interest me. This went on for months, and then one day he said something I couldn't ignore, "You want to impact 30 kids or 800? I will hire someone to fill the position and when they aren't as smart as you or don't move in a way you like, you better just eat it". I didn't admit it at the time but this resonated with me like a new Meek Mill song dropping on a summer day.[2] (For those who don't get the reference, it's a feeling similar to seeing Micheal Jackson perform live for one more night.) The idea that being in a position of leadership would mean being in control of how students learned and received support excited me. I also know that although I didn't want to lead, I knew how to on the technical side. While apprehensive, I was also extremely privileged that he valued what I believed to be best for kids. To this day, I am enamored by his leadership and his ability to put up with someone like myself who can sometimes be downright difficult. He does so with grace, patience, and a dose of realness that I've never seen. I still have lots of work to do as my idea of a good time is a book, Teddy Pendergrass, and fuzzy socks, but what matters is I have Principal Kane's unwavering support and belief in my ability.

I provide this tangent to illustrate that Principal Kane's belief in me and willingness to support me as a mentor in spite of my sometimes-dogmatic ways are due to the fact that he (I hope) believes my value system aligns with his and what he wants for the community. I also believe *he* believes I am capable. I am someone who believes it is important to get involved in "good trouble" for the sake of kids and families. I am also unapologetic about equity centeredness in my leadership and instruction. I follow through with this as a model for culturally responsive practices. I am a deep thinker, many times biting off more than I can chew, but always see the task to its completion. Principal Kane is all of those things, and he possesses a superpower like no other—seeing potential in others and providing them exactly with the support they need. Now before you all start looking him up and thinking we have a stress-free mentor/mentee relationship, that idea is completely false. We disagree on things all the time! The beauty in his leadership is that he cares deeply about transparency, taking care of people, and letting others know they have value in all spaces. I say this to say if you are a leader whose core values are clear and present and you walk in them every day, like-minded people will gravitate toward you and respect your leadership. Be a model of your leadership or as the Migos said, "Walk it like you talk it!" Not just because you are a leader in title but because you are able to be a model for what you believe in. Your leadership team should be a reflection of that even if the message will be communicated a little differently. A leader who is culturally responsive doesn't shy away from the unpleasantries of working with adults. It's easy to label someone as "difficult" and admonish them, but what if that difficult person is the answer to a challenge your school has? There will be people whose demeanor, leadership style, and core values just make them bad vibes for a community. However, you have to take into account if the presenting affect is a dealbreaker or if the person is in need of mentoring and reflection. You also have to know if *you* are the person to help them do the work. Here's an inquiry cycle you can go through to determine if it's worth the investment:

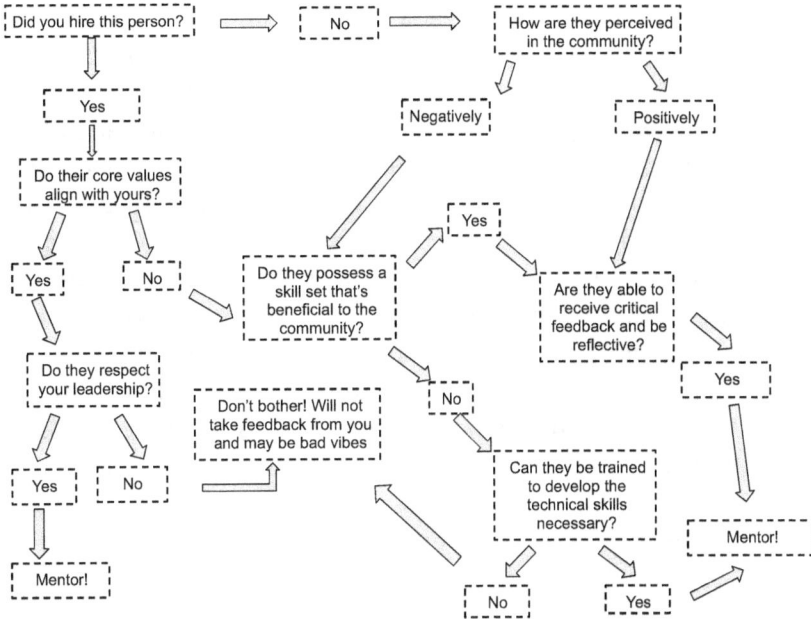

FIGURE 6.1 This is a flowchart for deciding if you have the capacity to mentor someone based on their relationship with you and the community.

In order for you to mentor someone or help them be reflective about their potential leadership in the community, they have to value and respect your ideals. Not just because you are the principal but at your core. As a Black woman, I value and respect Principal Kane's leadership because he has been a consistent advocate for what he believes in, in all spaces. This was evident when I was a teacher and is still true as an administrator under his leadership. One of his core values is meeting people where they are and seeing their humanity. He will help people with being reflective but does so by being vulnerable about his own leadership challenges. One day while I was still a teacher, I led a professional development for the staff. Our focus was Black and Brown children and how we were addressing their needs as the data showed this was our group that needed the most support at the time. I had all my notes, all of the technical things I wanted to say, and then unintentionally got deep into my feelings and made some people uncomfortable. I facilitated while being in my feelings and saw what kids had told me about their mistreatment instead of the goal of the professional learning. When my facilitation was questioned because "they did not want to hear the message from me" (actual quote), Principal Kane, then Assistant Principal Kane, spoke up and out for me. Not to defend me being in my feelings but to push that person to evaluate the why and what made them uncomfortable about the message. He also spoke to me one-on-one about the internal work I needed to do not as a means of invalidating my feelings but to get into the practice of calling people in as a lever for impacting real change. If I did not see Principal Kane as someone who believed in me and also walked in his values, I might have missed the message or dismissed it completely. I say that to say the person you choose to mentor has to value your personhood, core values, and leadership in order for the relationship to be successful.

If You Get to Choose, Count Your Blessings and Be Intentional!

Many people will not get to choose who their leadership teams consist of. We will talk about that more in the next section. If you have the liberty of hiring your administrative team as well as instructional leadership team, I will stress having a clear understanding of who you are, including strengths and weaknesses. Focusing on strengths and weaknesses will allow you to determine if potential candidates can fill a gap that is integral to the functioning of the school community. For example, as an English language arts (ELA)/English teacher, I am strong in that area and I have the prior knowledge and training to lead that team if necessary. If I am looking for someone to run the math department or special education department, candidates should possess the technical skills necessary to engage in this work deeply. Knowing our leadership areas of strength as well as areas of growth is also important for core value work and temperament. If I am a leader who tends to be reclusive and curt, as a culturally responsive leader I should want someone to balance that with warmth and openness as a natural part of their personality as the end goals are a positive school culture and support for stakeholders.

Of course, this does not absolve me from also working on my leadership style and making attempts to be warm and welcoming. Introspection is a necessary part of selecting leaders and is a culturally responsive practice, but this is not often discussed. It is easy to be a leader who sees their title as a rationale for making decisions in isolation or needing to be consulted for any and everything happening in a school building. It is much more difficult to ask, "Why would someone want to work for *me*? What do I offer as a leader? What are my areas of growth? How can these be supported alongside the leadership of another?" When you interview or are looking to appoint a leader, it is important to have questions that are strategic and that speak to your core values and will elicit telling responses. The questions will vary depending on the position being offered but should all provide a lens into your leadership style and non-negotiables. Hiring or appointing a teacher leader is different from hiring for an administrative position, but the ends are the same. You are looking for an advocate for students who is able to be reflective and meet the needs of the community at large in spite of their own temporary discomfort or opinions. Here are some culturally responsive questions I would ask with my core values being culturally responsive pedagogy, equity, and trust:

- What are you looking for in a leader?
- What are you looking for in a school community?
- What do you value most about working with adults?
- A staff member has come to you in confidence about not being comfortable teaching about the Holocaust. How do you respond?
- The principal had to make a hard decision that had a negative impact. You did not agree with this decision. How do you communicate about it when asked by staff?
- A non-negotiable for me is communication—good or bad—tell me about a time you struggled to communicate and how you handled it.
- Do you foresee working with (insert group or demographic)? If so, why? What are they?
- What is your understanding of culturally responsive-sustaining education (CRSE)?

While these questions are not foolproof indicators of a person's viewpoint on leadership, they will elicit a glimpse into how they handle adversity, challenging staff, and relationships. These are all important elements of leadership as they are areas where I try to be intentional about developing myself. Being a leader requires continual evaluation and "checking" of one's self and belief systems. You want to hire or appoint someone who is aligned with your beliefs but also has their own core values and non-negotiables. Being culturally responsive in choosing leaders means that you are up-front about your belief systems and non-negotiables yet malleable in the face of new ideas. Your leadership is deeply rooted in your beliefs, but you are also able to let someone else run the ship without looking over their shoulder. If you were indisposed for a month, would the culture thrive or disintegrate? A culturally responsive leader trusts who they've selected to lead and walks alongside them as well as behind. If you always need to be in front of the camera, check in with yourself and reflect on why.

TABLE 6.1 Leadership Evaluation Check-In

- What do you value most?
- When presented with a challenge in the community, do these values waiver?
- Do these values show up in all of your decisions or just some?
- Do you trust others to lead? Why or why not?
- What are your greatest areas of growth? How do you go about addressing these?
- If you asked staff, would they agree you embody these values you selected?

So You Adopted an OPP!?

"Opp" is a slang term which is short for "opposition."[3] If someone is an "opp," that means they stand to present significant challenges to your agenda or goals as they are not in support of what you have envisioned. In some cases, they may intentionally derail initiatives. In most leadership scenarios, you have adopted a team and have no say in who leads what teams. Why do I refer to them as "opps?" Because anyone who stands in the way of what you envision for children and families is literally *opposing* your mission. (The young people in my life also tell me if you don't have opps, you aren't doing something right!) While their suggestion is to "flex on them" by "doing your big one," we need to understand that opposition and dissent are necessary.

If you're a principal, that means your administrative team has already been in place, and if you are an assistant principal, that means the teacher leadership teams you will oversee have already been set in place. The challenge in this is if there is a clear need for disruption or a change in culture, you as the new leader cannot walk in and abolish what has always been. I mean, you can, but it comes at the risk of your school's culture being established with you as a tyrant and having a bias. This is a terrible way to introduce yourself. The best way to engage in this scenario is to be a listener, ask lots of questions, and use the VIBE: School Culture model as an assessment of the school needs (see Chapter 3). While it will take time to earn trust and respect as a new school leader, it will be worth having stakeholders see you as someone who is invested in keeping systems and structures that work versus trying to abandon all things you do not agree with. Now here's the quiet part out loud: Some things need to just be blown UP. Yelling at kids and creating an unsafe environment, avoidance of certain parent groups, being on the phone watching TikToks instead of teaching. These are extreme examples but they are all things that cannot wait for warmth, inquiry, and feedback. Address challenges that are immediate concerns in real time and play surgeon with all of the delicacies of leadership and culture that can handle a slower more methodical approach. Something else a culturally responsive school leader would do is get to know the leadership team on a one-on-one level. I'm not suggesting taking them out to dinner, or maybe I am. What it looks like for you will vary, but there is great value in taking time to get to know who the people on your leadership team are, as this will help you track and trace their belief systems. I truly believe most people are well intended, and apprehension or refusal is usually the by-product of something larger like fear, insecurity, low-self-esteem or belief in one's own capacity. A prime example was my own reluctance to become a leader as I had a fear of being seen as competent. Being a leader who is aware that "Big Bad Wolves" manifest in the lives of others in the form of aversion allows you to support them in ways they did not know they needed. Most of the time, your "opps" aren't actually oppositional. They are just dealing with their own unsurfaced and unaddressed challenges. For all those who do actually have "opps" in their leadership spaces, you will always have to be intentional about creating clear expectations and systems for accountability. This can be aligned with data outcomes, school culture outcomes, as well as reception data from the streets. Showing that their affect and leadership do not align with the school goals or culture and the impact this has on the community will be the best route for you if you ever have to move into a more discipline-oriented approach. Always ground your observations and conclusions in outcomes for the community aligned with their belief systems.

TABLE 6.2 Opp Scenario

One of your administrators does not believe in the advisory program you want to roll out, and they are quietly supporting teachers who don't want it, either. Student surveys show they want better relationships with one another. You believe advisory is the answer as it is geared toward socio-emotional wellness and building relationships in smaller groups. The administrator in charge has been undermining the program by telling teachers they don't see the purpose, that it is a waste of instructional time, and that kids aren't going to go. This is in clear opposition to your leadership and the school goals as the program arose from the voice of students and most staff are excited to begin. So what do you do?

Head: The administrative member is undermining a school goal that will benefit the young people in your building.

Heart: Core values are student voice and positive relationships, truth, and transparency.

Hands: Talking to the staff member about this will either have them be defensive *or* reveal their true reason for apprehension.

In the example above, if the staff member is expressing anxiety through vocal discontent to others, there are ways to address this. The first way to address this is to look inward. Why didn't they feel they could tell you about their uneasiness or uncertainty? Do they need support with implementation? The second way to address this is inquiry as the apprehension could also be due to their internal value system. Do they not feel like students should have a voice? Are they pro-anything that is easy for them and the program deviates from that? If the latter of the two is the problem, then you know the person on your team has some core work to do *or* they are bad vibes in the community and may need to find another. In either case, you always want to start with introspection and inquiry.

Get Granular

Who Leads the Intimate Teams?

A school building has lots of teams to be run, and each of them should have a point person at the helm. For example, each content team should have a leader who is not administrative, and each team that engages students and families—such as the parent engagement team or student council team—should have leads who support its day-to-day functioning. While it may be difficult to determine who should lead what as sometimes there is more than one worthy candidate, not appointing one speaks volumes but not about what you'd think. While appointing someone may illustrate an element of favoritism or a sort of endorsement, if you will, not appointing someone can mean that as a school leader you don't value that team. Created a new initiative to implement a college and career program but didn't have anyone overseeing it? There will be little to no success. Created a new literacy initiative but the person in charge doesn't follow up or follow through? You as the leader must not be supporting them, or the person in charge doesn't care. For the streets, this ultimately means the program isn't to be seriously followed. For all of the aforementioned reasons, it is important to have a person to be responsible for communication, updates, and support and to report the overall vibe about the initiative or plan. Without this, visions and initiatives are just checkboxes to show others you have things in place. What good are they if they are not supported? The value lies in the integration and implementation of the strategies or initiatives you wish to introduce. Having a point person indicates you care about the work and its outcome. In regard to follow-up, it is important that as a culturally responsive leader you remember "If not me, then who?" There are many ways a school leader can present themselves as "change agents" without truly providing the support necessary to create systems and structures for impactful and positive change. Below are some examples of the teams and leads necessary for a culturally responsive team lead approach. Implementation is like buying a car. You can pay handsomely for it, but if the maintenance is not consistent, it will slowly break down and be much more costly in the long term.

TABLE 6.3 Teams and Leadership: Capacity Building

- *Content Teams*
  - Ideally, each content area should have a chair and a coach to support the department.
  - The lead also coordinates the meetings and elicits support of other staff members in providing support and professional learning.
  - The team leader is not part of the administrative team but supports the administrative goals and communicates with the administrator overseeing the department about needs and challenges.
  - They should not be viewed as administrators and are not reporting agents. They are a safe space for the team to challenge and question any and all things aligned with the initiative.
- *Guidance Team*
  - There should be someone overseeing and supporting the guidance team as they not only are working with caseloads but also are supporting the socio-emotional goals of the school for all students.
  - They should be aware of instructional goals and supports as well as the core values of the school community and imbue these when they meet with students.
- *Grade Teams*
  - These teams are responsible for the day-to-day planning and activities of students. It is important for someone to oversee classroom interactions, hallway interactions, and overall grade expectations to ensure that they align with the mission and vision of the school community.
- *Student Leadership Teams*
  - There should be a staff member supporting student led events, initiatives, and programs that are part of the community.
  - This person aligns student goals with overall school goals.
  - Student-run leadership with teacher support
- *Parent Engagement Team*
  - Team members are responsible for being the intermediary between the school and families.
  - This includes events, potential decisions, curriculum and instruction, and much more.
  - Should ideally include parents who help run it

How do they lead the intimate teams?

It is not enough just to have someone appointed to support or lead a team. *How* they lead is just as important. You can have someone who is instructionally sound and knows everything there is to know about the content area. If their team doesn't like them, there will be no transfer or building of knowledge. "Like" is subjective as I am sure we don't all "like" everyone we work with, but it is important for the team to find value in and trust the person appointed and believe that they have their head, heart, and goals in the right place. You want to appoint someone who not only is intelligent and technically sound but also has the ability to read a room, assess and be reflective, apologize when necessary, and deliver your message in a way that allows people to hear it out before buying in. There is nothing worse than having your message muddled or disregarded because your appointee didn't believe in it or didn't communicate it in a way that allowed for discourse and inquiry. Yes, you are the school leader, so it can be asserted that you should be delivering your own messages, but I would argue you should be the last person to deliver the message depending on what it is. If the message is about a major shift or disruption, you as the leader should be delivering the message as change and culture shifts should be supported or rolled-out top-down. This allows you to provide a rationale and justification for core value alignment and potential outcomes. Knowing that the principal believes in the initiative or is the guiding force behind it sets an important tone. In other cases, your positionality may automatically be an off-ramp for some, and despite your best efforts, the message may become lost in your presence and role. An integral part of culturally responsive leadership is giving people the space and opportunity to hear a message or proposal and critique and interrogate it at will, without fear of retribution or judgment. I am a person who needs to ask questions in order to process. Would I as a teacher have asked my boss the same questions about a project that I would ask a peer I trust? Probably not. This is why it is important to have people with boots on the ground who can answer the tough questions as both a peer who will be working alongside them and a connector who has access to information and depth others may not. Your role is to ensure that the message or initiative, as well as the rationale behind it, is clear to those you choose to appoint. So long as they are asking you the tough questions and have the rationale behind why, you are setting yourself up for success with any implementation you desire. This is not foolproof, but if your squad has the best possible information, they are able to show up in spaces in a way that is supportive for others. Here is an example of why it is important to appoint leaders to various spaces:

TABLE 6.4 Incoming Freshman Example

Incoming Freshman Example:
You want the 9th-grade teacher team to host a welcome reception for all of the freshmen. You'd like this to be led by the seniors of the building for a "mentor" experience.

Option 1:	**Option 2**:
You don't have someone supporting the planning for the freshman team. This leaves you to be the intermediary between the 9th-grade team and those who will help with the senior planning. For this to be done effectively, there will need to be multiple meetings and planning sessions. As the principal, you are always time-strapped. Is this feasible? What was the intended outcome? What is the potential impact?	You appoint a team lead for both the 9th- and 12th-grade teams You meet with them to talk over vision, goals, and outcomes. They then lead each of their teams in planning to serve as the intermediary. As they have met with you, they can problem-solve and thought-partner with one another for success. This also provides the opportunity for them to take the lead and add some seasoning to the overall plan!

In option 1, you are left to be the creative director of the planning process. While the idea may have been yours, it is not realistic for you to continually meet for planning sessions. This level of integration in the planning also makes you the determining factor for all decisions versus allowing teachers and teams to let their own ideas flourish and benefit the community. In option 2, you set the expectation that the event takes place, show support for it, and let those with boots on the ground make decisions about what they will ultimately have to execute. You are showing trust and support for an event that will be a bright spot for the community, all while stepping aside and letting those you trust lead.

How Do YOU Support?

We've established that as a leader you will not always support the team personally but whom you choose to do so matters. It is not enough to just appoint someone, they also need to be supported through the allocation of time, feedback, and other needs based on the feedback from their teams. Capacity building extends beyond your leadership teams—it extends to what all community members are learning on a continual basis. A culturally responsive school leader feeds the streets at all levels and ensures that even those on the leadership team are continually developing themselves and their practice for the betterment of the community. Just as school leaders continually reflect and grow, so should staff, students, and families. Below are some questions to ask yourself as a leader about support you are offering holistically as well as for leadership:

TABLE 6.5 Leadership Support Inquiry

- How often do you provide professional development for staff?
  - Is it differentiated based on needs? Content area? Strengths?
  - Is it led by consultants? Other staff? Yourself?
    - What are the dangers of leading the professional learning yourself?
- How do you continue to develop veteran teachers?
- How do you support teachers who are new to the profession?
- Where do you program your strongest teachers?
  - Are they working with the students who are most vulnerable and in need?
  - Do they teach only advanced courses and gifted & talented?
- Are there opportunities for families to receive professional learning on school-related things such as implementation of a new curriculum, adoption of a new behavior system, and inclusion of equity work?
  - If not, why?
  - Are there family leadership opportunities?
- Do your appointed leaders have time to consort with one another?
  - About challenges that arise?
  - Dissent and pushback?
  - Positive feedback?
  - To plan and support their teams?
  - To invest in their own professional learning around pedagogy?
  - To invest in their own professional learning around their leadership?
  - To reflect on their Head, Heart, and Hands?

More Programming for Success

Your school's program and professional learning are also indicators of how you've built capacity and imbued your core values into the community. The instructional program is an integral part of ensuring that teams and team leads have what they need to be successful. In the example of the 9th-grade welcome, teachers and staff have to have time to meet and do the work required for planning. The same is true for new programs or initiatives. While time is the only commodity we don't get any more of, what you do with it can set you up for success or derail your plans. Is there time for students to commiserate outside of academic spaces about their feelings and social challenges? If so, have you programmed time for their teachers to be adequately trained? Is there a new program for college and career readiness that students can take but they'd need to stay for an extra period? Have you reworked the program to be reflective of this change and included teacher voice in the process? Do all parents and families know of this opportunity as well as how to subscribe?

All of these questions will depend upon your community, but what I want to impress upon you is the importance of ensuring that there are supports in place in the form of people whose leadership and lens you trust. Your team is an extension of your leadership, and you are only as strong as your most burnt-out or confused leader. Set your school culture up for success by doing the "people work" necessary at all levels. Each school's schedule will vary based on geographic location, but there should always be time for the following:

→ Vertical teacher meeting time
→ Horizontal teacher meeting time

- → Department meeting time (content, special education, English as a new language [ENL], etc.)
- → Grade team meeting
- → Coaching time/meetings
- → Co-teaching meeting times
- → Student-facing time for socio-emotional learning
- → Time for non-academic engagement (such as electives or other programs)

This list looks impossible and you may be saying to yourself, "Ain't nobody got time for that!" Each of these areas speaks to a different team or area of need within your community. Whatever you choose to omit in the interest of preserving time will ultimately require those teams to be strong enough to go without or collaborate on their own. For example, omitting time for departments to meet means there is a risk of different grade teams veering off the curriculum due to lack of clear expectations around cohesion. Potential unintended consequence? That new V.I.B.E. model for culturally responsive curriculum modification can't get its legs. Don't provide time for coaches to meet with one another? There will not be any conversation around challenges present within classrooms across various departments and grades. This can lead to every coach working on their own island, operating from what they believe to be best. Part of being a culturally conscious leader means starting with the best intentions in mind and then scaling back when you absolutely must. Use your instructional program as a lever for supporting initiatives and providing space for collaboration. The more time and space there is for discourse and unpacking of challenges, the more solutions will be found. This allows for more voices to aid in the process. After all, you are more of a maestro than the person playing the strings.

Capacity Building: That's Your People? Application and Materials

Whose Mans is This?
Capacity Building

Entering	Emerging	Applying	Deepening
The program is driven by student needs. Each team should report to me as the leader of the building for their inquiries and needs.	The program is created with teacher meeting time included. Each team should manage themselves as this is how people learn best and it builds interdependence. Team leaders serve as the "lead learners" and help lead others.	The program is created with students, teachers, and coaches in mind, centering collaboration and reflection time. Each team has an appointed "point person" to support and serve as an intermediary between administration. Team leaders are also continually supported through professional learning.	The program is a reflection of my core values as a leader and that of the school community. Team leaders are a reflection of stakeholders in different roles, not just administrative. Team leaders are provided with frequent inquiry cycles from teams to reflect on their vibe.

Activity

Use the information below to determine what needs to be set in place to address the challenge presented.

A teacher on the special education team has surfaced the following concerns:

- The administrator overseeing the department does not have a background in special education and is advising things that are compliance violations.
- The teacher has spoken to the administrator and expressed these concerns, and the administrator is apologetic. They express being very busy overseeing more than one team.
- The teacher has 15 years of experience in special education and is knowledgeable, and the department respects their voice.
- The teacher does not want to lead but feels like someone should as they are frustrated with the current circumstances.

Scenario-Based Practice:

Building Student Capacity

Use the scenario below to craft a response to the student concern that will show you building their capacity and using a culturally responsive leadership lens.

A student comes to you after having spoken to their teacher and assistant principal about the lunch being served. The student states that the snacks provided are cold, the milk is frozen, and the food choices do not reflect the needs or interests of students in the building. The student wants to know what can be done and what you as the principal are going to do.

Think: *Whom do you need to tap into to address the challenge presented? How do you support or cultivate their activism?*

"What Keeps you Grounded?"
Readings and Vibes

Notes

1. The term "Imposter Syndrome" was coined by Dr. Pauline Clance and Dr. Suzanne Imes. It speaks to a feeling of inadequacy even in the face of accolades and success.
2. Mill's "Dreams and Nightmares" (2012) is still the song that puts me in "go mode" for all things. It's my leadership song that gets me in the zone and ready to tackle the shenanigans that sometimes come with the job. I encourage every leader to have one of their own!
3. See definition of "opp" online at Urban Dictionary (n.d.): https://www.urbandictionary.com/define.php?term=opp

Additional Reading

Sinek, S. (2009). *Start with why: How great leaders inspire everyone to take action.* Portfolio/Penguin.

7

Data and Progress Monitoring

Numbers Don't Lie, Right?

Lisa Delpit spoke to my soul when she stated,

> assessment is a lot trickier than we think, especially if the children we are assessing are not from the same culture as the test makers…many teachers unfamiliar with the language, the metaphors, or the environment of the children they teach may easily underestimate the children's competence.
>
> (137–138)

Measurements and assessments are a large part of how a school leader is evaluated. You are a reflection of the exams and assessments that students take, surveys that teachers and stakeholders respond to, and the informal feedback you receive from the community at large. The reality is you cannot always control the exact outcomes of the data. Yes, you can plan for what you'd like to see and make strategic moves aligned with that, but there are things that will force you to pivot and disrupt plans you might have had in place. It is important to understand you are not exclusively a reflection of your data, but how you respond and what you do with it are what you will be remembered for. There are two very important areas that are integral to understanding assessment data, but these areas do not always have clear policies. Attendance impacts how students are learning as well as grades. Having a clear, equity-driven assessment grading policy provides information on whether students are accessing what they are being taught. Let's first discuss the different forms of assessment and their impact.

Data Measures

Formal Measures

Data comes "formally" and "informally". Formal data measures are often viewed as objective in that everyone in the state or jurisdiction takes them, they are created with the standards aligned with the state, and all students are given the same amount of time to take them, with the exception of those who are allocated additional time due to having varied learning needs. The creation, conditions, and administration of these exams make it so that you as the school leader are provided with everything needed in advance for students to be successful. Right? Wrong. There are unforeseen challenges that present themselves in the form of community needs, funding for school programs, and teaching staff skill sets. These are things that are not accounted for in formal data, but the measures remain nonetheless. The data being collected for your school is formal if it allows for you to be compared with schools with your likeness in terms of grade band, region/district, and content area. In New York State, examples of these formal measures are the end-of-year State Exams in English language arts (ELA)/English and math for elementary and middle school as well as the Regents examinations for high schools. These tests are summative and put a school on display for its ability to help students pass them or inability to do so. The reality is that formal measures are important as they do provide a lens on what needs to be strengthened in your community or what you are already doing well. These measures extend to surveys that students are asked to take in regard to their socioemotional wellness and their experiences in school so long as they are provided by the locale. As easy as it is to focus on the things you cannot control in relation to these measures (if you're type-A like me and take all feedback to heart), it is important to use the data as a lever for improvement in all spaces. There are always extenuating factors for formal data measures not lining up with what their expectations are. However, the circumstances should not deter you from being reflective and moving to impact change. Two things can be true at the same time: formal data measures can be better than what is reported *and* the extenuating circumstances impacting them need to be addressed. Education is the only arena where children can "fail" and those involved keep their jobs. Some are even lauded for being "of service" to the community. This notion is even more true when it comes to failing children of color. The lack of accountability is alarming and shows up in the form of a push for more "remediation" programs or quick fixes for children of urban communities without providing additional services for families at large. What is missing is a form of accountability. There are always challenges to academic success, but I promise you they are not driven by the negative mental models aligned with student ability. Schmoker's teaching practices for accountability include

> being clear about what is to be learned and assessed, clearly explicating and carefully teaching the criteria by which student work will be scored, and using assessments to evaluate a lesson's effectiveness to make adjustments on the basis of results.
>
> (Delpit 141–142)

These practices exist within assessment but aren't always explicitly followed. Formal measures can be disheartening as they often focus on performance and not growth. Examples of this for New York State would be the state exams in ELA and mathematics. Students' scores fall on a scale of 1–4. If a student goes from a 1.2 to a 1.4, this is growth and should be seen as a lever for success. So often formal measures decide whether you *are* or *aren't*, reducing students to such objective measures is cold and doesn't take into account incremental progress. As in an evaluation that is "satisfactory" or "unsatisfactory," there is no room for discussion or next steps in the scoring. The assertion is "you're doing okay" or "just do better!"

One form of formal data that is important to school culture but is sometimes overlooked is attendance. Attendance is a reflection of the status of your school population and their needs. The goal is to have all of your students attending on time every day as this indicates one of two things. One, students and families are aligned in their belief about school being important and ensure that students are present for their learning. Two, students enjoy their experience in the community and are coming on time and daily willingly because they want to be part of what's happening in the building and value the time with their friends and community. Having attendance that is less than favorable doesn't always mean there is an issue with your school culture; it can mean there are familial challenges that impede daily student attendance and punctuality. You also want to know this so you can help support students and families holistically. Examples of this include having to drop off a sibling in the morning, students having to get themselves ready and needing support for waking up, or just the need for transportation if they live farther away from the community. Formal attendance data is reflected in your absenteeism rate. This would be a percentage for the school community, and if you are being culturally responsive with the data, it should also be broken down by grade level, race, economic status, and learning ability status (English as a new language [ENL], integrated co-teaching [ICT], special education, etc.). This will allow you to have a layered approach to addressing attendance concerns and the root causes of them. If these challenges present themselves within your attendance data, it is also important to determine if there are informal measures that can be assessed to address root causes. This is listening to the "V" Voices in Chapter 3. The focus on attendance and not grades as the primary data point is important as you need students in school consistently to educate! If there is a disruption in attendance—special education students missing more time in school than others, for example—it is important for you as a culturally responsive leader to know this and address it as the primary form of assessment as you cannot support students who aren't there. Schools should be sanctuaries and places of safety for young people, and you want your community to feel like a place they don't want to leave. You also want to support families and the community at large, and attendance audits allow you to provide outreach and support for those who may not ask for it. It may also unearth information like Nasir being up playing on his game system until 2 a.m. and he would like to be part of the gaming club—an incentive that can be used to call in, not admonish or call out.

Grading is Important, Too!

In my teacher preparation program for my master's degree in education, we did not spend much time learning about grading. We barely spent time learning about how to be effective teachers. What we did learn about were all the theorists and their impact on education and student learning. Of course, this was more important than learning how to actually teach, right? When I stepped into a classroom, I figured out *how* to teach from the great models around me who explained you need boots-on-the-ground experience to learn how to teach as the theorists and teacher tricks are cool but if kids don't like or respect you all the strategies will not be effective in application. What surprised me most was that grading was left up to my teacher discretion. Yes, the school had a policy for grading in terms of weights and percentages for assignments and tasks for each department. But I was allowed to grade with no oversight and had the final say. Was this explicitly stated? Of course not. Grading is an unspoken "teacher practice" that allows lots of room for subjectivity. That kid whose overall grade was an 88 and they tried really hard in class? Let's give them the extra 2 points to make it a 90. That kid who never tried and walked around the room all period got a 63? I guess he will just fail the course. Grading is not an objective practice, even though it should be. It should also be asset-based and ensure that students are learning, not just complying with behavioral demands and rote skills. To ensure that our grading doesn't fall victim to the objective formal measures which reduce students to an arbitrary number, we need a system that is equitable and allows for conversations centered on growth and attainment of skills. We will talk more about mastery-based grading (MBG). First let's talk about tasks and expectations.

Start with Norming

One thing we did explicitly in my department that was an integral part of grading was "norming" our responses. In this process, we looked at the task and determined what an acceptable grade-level answer would be for the question posed. We also discussed grade-level variations of the responses aligned with the task and questions. This allowed us to determine what learning gaps there were and what answers we would collectively accept. Me grading over my free period and my colleague grading over her Saturday didn't exactly allow us time to talk over responses as we graded. The danger of this is if we had different expectations around an acceptable response, our students in different classes would have different bars to reach. Norming provides a skeleton for appropriate responses and an outline for those that are not aligned with expectations at all. This is a strong and purposeful practice as norming will mean that the accepted response will be the same across grades (vertical alignment) and this allows us to know where we as teachers need to pivot our instructional practices to provide for more access. An example of this is as follows:

TABLE 7.1 Toni Morrison Task Example

Student Task Example *Beloved**
Task: Students will read *Beloved* by Toni Morrison and write an essay where they explain the significance of relationships between mothers and daughters.
Be sure to cite evidence and use analysis to support your claims.

* *Beloved* by Toni Morrison is one of many books on the list to be banned because of its themes around slavery and challenging descriptions. If you've never read it, it is a must-read.

To the question above, teachers should have an understanding of what they believe is a developed, grade-level response to the question, what is below grade level or underdeveloped, and what demonstrates there needing to be a complete reteach of the skills or materials utilized. The task requires multiple literacy skills as students are asked to demonstrate comprehension of the text (secondary skill), and they are asked to make an inference about Sethe's decision to kill her daughter as well as the driving force behind it (primary skill). Students are also asked to write a cohesive and intelligible response to the question, citing evidence and analyzing the text. All of these are measurable and transferable skills that students can use at various grade levels. Given the themes of the text, *Beloved* is usually a course taught in Advanced Placement (AP) high school courses or at the college level. While the depth of the writing will be reflective of the grade level, the task is the same. Before we talk Mastery Based Grading (MBG), let's first unpack the task and where the misconceptions are.

TABLE 7.2 Toni Morrison Student Responses

Possible Student Examples
Student C: Though her act was heinous and leads to her haunting, Sethe engaged in the deepest level of love and sacrifice but does so at the unintentional cost of her relationship with her family.
Student B: Sethe killed her daughter because she did not want one.
Student A: Sethe killed because she saw others being killed and just acted out of anger.

The student with the "beginning" response demonstrates that there may be a comprehension issue with the text as Sethe did not want her daughter to suffer the atrocities of slavery and this was made clear in the text. Without getting in my ELA teacher mode, the student with the "developing" response demonstrates deep comprehension of the text because they address the conundrum Sethe was placed in when giving birth to her daughter. The response also addresses the fact that the act in itself was not one easily decided for Sethe, thus setting them up with a claim for an essay that addresses the difficulty between mothers and daughters when difficult decisions have to be made. There are a variety of answers that fall in between a developed response and one that is not yet there, so how is a teacher team to determine what answers are acceptable or at which level they should be rated? Ultimately, the goal is to assign grades, right? The answer to these questions is rubric alignment in MBG.

In alignment with culturally responsive practices, MBG focuses on students "mastering" skills aligned with their grade-level competencies. Whereas numerical grading can focus on other outcomes and leave room for that elusive subjectivity, MBG allows students to demonstrate proficiency with standards and skills for their grade level.

Grading SHOULD be culturally responsive

In his book *Grading for Equity*, Joel Feldman (2019) states that grading should be equitable, and he provides three pillars for this:

> Grading should be "Accurate, Bias-Resistant, and Motivational" (Feldman, 2019: 66). Accurate grading ensures that grades are clear and not confusing for students. Bias-resistant grading provides students with "an opportunity to succeed regardless of privilege. These are grading practices that counteract our biases we bring into classrooms aligned to race, gender, income, first language, or special needs. Motivational grades serve to intrinsically motivate and promote a growth mindset."
>
> (Feldman, 2019: 66)

Dr. Gloria Ladson-Billings's pillar of academic success states that "students need literacy, numeracy, technological, social, and political skills in order to be active participants in democracy" (Ladson-Billings, 1995). This aligns with the tenets of MBG and Feldman's pillars because students have specific learning targets and tasks that are aligned with their content areas. These tasks provide a clear and transparent method for obtaining the skills or reaching the goals for the standard being addressed. MBG also provides students with rubrics that are asset-oriented with actionable next steps. In traditional grading, the outcomes are often driven by subjective numerical values for students. Rubrics are an important part of mastery and ensure that the measures for mastering the standards are clear to ensure student success. Here is an example of a mastery rubric versus a traditional grading template:

TABLE 7.3 Grading Examples: Mastery versus Traditional

	Mastery-Based Rubric Examples			Traditional Numerical Grading Scale	
Example 1	Beginning	Developing	Mastery	96%–100%	A
Example 2	Working Towards	Meeting	Exceeding	86%–95%	B
				76%–85%	C
				65%–75%	D
				0%–55%	F

In the MBG scale provided, students would be provided with criteria for each of the areas. This allows for students to have an understanding of why they are at the level ascribed to them on their assignment as well as how to advance to the next level. In each area, the student can determine what they are missing in order to reach the next rubric area. In an ideal scenario, teachers would meet with students at various points in the year to conference and discuss a student's mastery level for various standards. This is all aimed at building student agency and having them take ownership over their own learning or, as Zaretta Hammond calls it, creating "independent learners" (Hammond, 2015). Here's what that may look like based on a specific standard for literacy:

TABLE 7.4 Mastery Rubric Example

Mastery Rubric:
Standard 1: Read closely to determine what the text says explicitly/implicitly and make logical inferences from it; cite specific textual evidence when writing or speaking to support your conclusions.

Beginning	Developing	Mastering
Claim provided is a stated fact. Evidence was a paraphrase, not a direct citation.	Claim provided hinted to an inference but was not made clear, and evidence cited was specific to the claim provided but claim is not direct.	Claim provided is driven by context clues and inferring; and evidence cited directly supports the claim provided.

The rubric above provides students with the opportunity to move from "beginning" to "mastering" through deepening their understanding of the criteria. In the *Beloved* example, the student in the "student A (Beginning)" needed to go back and make a claim that is driven by their observations of the text in conjunction with one another versus what is explicitly stated. There are also socio-emotional benefits to MBG and education. MBG, if done well, includes rubrics for work habits and areas that students often find are not rated as part of their learning. Habit evaluation through the use of rubrics provides students with an opportunity to receive feedback on the tertiary skills that are often precursors to their academic success. Examples of these habits are revisions after feedback, organization and timeliness, explaining versus repeating, and preparedness. While these skills are not rated or driven by "standards" per say, they are important as they teach students the necessary skills to help them advance and reach their academic goals through the support of their work habits and "habits" as a student. My own work habit area would be timeliness as I am a procrastinator who uses last-minute pressure to produce my best work! This often causes me stress and anxiety that could be avoided. The mastery process is aimed at ensuring that students possess the formula for their own academic success versus the educator being the arbitrator of said success. This turns the table and puts students in the owner's seat. Another large component of MBG is the fact there are multiple opportunities for students to demonstrate "mastery" of the standards within their learning. Each assignment should be tethered to specific standards that are repeated at multiple points throughout the year in both formal and informal tasks. This ensures that students are able to use different contexts to provide evidence of their learning. For example, in the rubric above, a student may have 7x to practice the skill of inferring and citing evidence. If they are "masters" in 5 out of the 7 attempts, they have demonstrated "mastery" of the skill. If they are averaging 4 developings, 2 beginners, and 1 master, I would argue the student is still in the developing stage as they have more consistently demonstrated being at that level over the course of the term/marking period. In each of these examples, though, students can refer to the rubric to determine what they need to do differently to move to the "mastery" stage. But what about feedback? Do the rubrics take the place of teacher feedback and next steps? Of course not. While the rubrics are there to aid students in understanding what they did well and how it aligned with the standard or what needs to be improved, the teacher feedback is an added layer that should help students understand what to do aligned with the specific context. If a student is "Developing" in the rubric above, the teacher feedback should be asset-based and specific to the content. More specifically, the student needed to form a claim that was inferential versus literal and needed to cite it in the text. Here's what that might sound like:

> Thank you for providing a strong point about the characters in the novel. You were able to speak clearly to the challenge the character endured. To move to the next level of master, talk about what that specific challenge revealed about the character. Hint: How did they handle the challenge you identified? What does that suggest about them and their approach to difficulty?

In this feedback example, I spoke to what the student did well and told them how to get to the next step with an asset-based approach that still required them to do the intellectual work. Feedback is an integral part of MBG and it is layered with the rubric, teacher feedback, and, most importantly, student self-assessment.

Ok, but how?
The one thing you as a school leader don't have control over are teacher's grades. Teachers are responsible for the grades that go onto report cards. Your role is to ensure that there is a clear grading policy that promotes student agency, removes subjectivity from the process, and removes compliance as a measure of academic success. Students in your community should know how to do better and what skills they can push themselves with as well as understand that grades are not a reward or punishment; rather, they are based on what one demonstrates through their evidence of learning. It will take time to implement an MBG system in your community as they are not often primarily utilized

within larger systems in the city, state, or district (despite the fact that there are rubrics for state and regional exams), so you may have to do lots of intellectual work with your team in order to understand how MBG aligns with your school ethos and current grading system. Start with one team that is the strongest and most willing to implement the grading system. Imbue this team with the foundational learning necessary to build understanding about the importance and purpose of the system. Don't rush the learning! There will need to be intrinsic value about MBG and culturally responsive pedagogical tenets in order for this system to be successful. The next step is to gradually aid the department in the implementation of rubrics driven by standards in each of the unit plans and instructional material throughout the year. This is where your instructional leads come into play in each of the departments. While implementation may be slow at first, it is important to do this work slowly and purposefully as there will be a learning curve for teachers, students, and families before it truly becomes part of the community. Having a model team that works purposefully to implement the system in their department, has a deep belief in culturally responsive-sustaining education (CRSE) and MBG, and can speak to challenges will aid in overall school implementation and support the integration overall.

Informal Measures

In my humble opinion, informal measures are the meat and potatoes of a school community. Just as informal measures in the classroom, such as questioning, allow a teacher to pivot and adjust their practice in real time to increase student achievement, for a school leader informal data provides a lens into things that are not usually referred to by the state/region as they can be subjective and will vary from school to school. These measures are also impacted by the years of service of the leadership at the school, student demographics, and engagement with families, and the list could go on. While these measures are also "unofficially" part of the state exam measures (the bottom of the iceberg), the cultivation and real work come from assessing these experiences and viewpoints at the ground level. In order to understand how to deeply impact what is seen and valued most, you have to first understand what to do with what you have been given. Informal measures are ones that will require lots of extra work on your part as they require a multi-layered approach. Stakeholders have to trust you and be willing to give honest feedback. They also have to believe that you are going to use their feedback to inform change. This process starts well before you desire to elicit data, and relationship building should always be at the forefront of your culturally responsive leadership. Once you decide you are ready to receive informal data, it should be layered and aligned with instructional goals, school climate, parent engagement, leadership style, and needs and supports. In our attendance data example, it would be important to use something such as a student and/or family survey to find out if students feel comfortable in the school building or if there are school culture–related things that are impacting their attendance and engagement. Examples of this would be questions below that speak to culture and affect as well as home life and personal challenges.

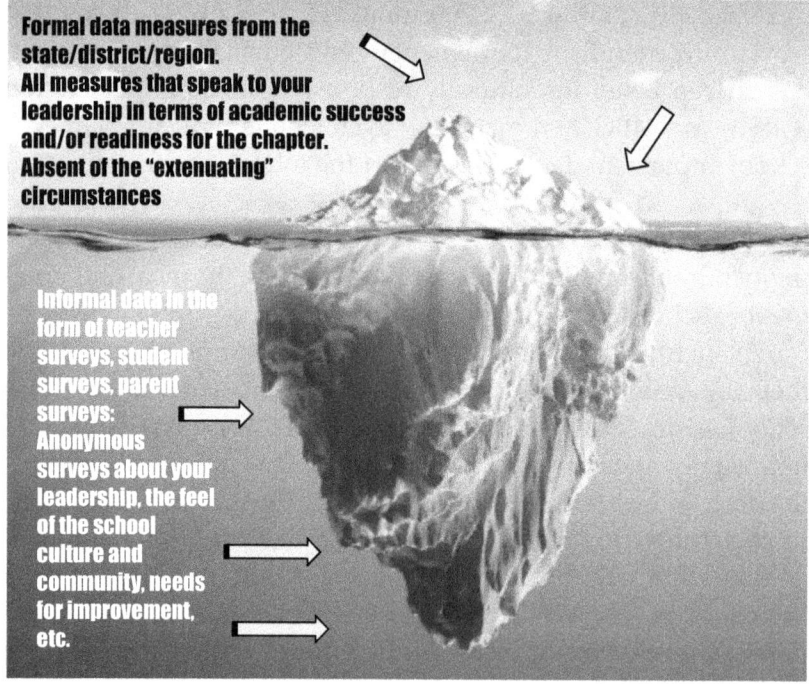

FIGURE 7.1 The iceberg represents data in a school community. At the tip of the iceberg are all of the formal and objective measures that often represent a school's "grade," and all of the extenuating informal factors are deeply lurking at the bottom. These must be addressed as well.

TABLE 7.5 Attendance Survey: Student-Facing

We've noticed that attendance and lateness are increasing/persisting across the school community. We want you here and hope you want to be here, so let's talk about what you need! This survey is anonymous and we want you to be as honest as possible.

- Do you have trouble getting to school on time? If so, why? How can we help?
- Do you have trouble getting to school in general? If so, why? How can we help?
- Do you feel safe in the classroom? In the school building? If not, where do you feel the most uncomfortable?
- Do you enjoy coming to school? If not, why? If so, what makes you happy here?
- What can we do to make you feel more welcomed and part of the community?
- How can we incentivize and recognize those who are consistently on time and present?

It is important that the questions be open-ended on this informal assessment as you want to give students the opportunity to provide answers that do not restrict them to a "yes" or "no" response. Short-response questions will allow for students to expand or explain their feelings and needs alongside attendance. It also ensures that you are not providing a survey that is rooted in assumptions about students and families. If you ask questions about student needs based on what you think or believe they need versus their actual desire it allows for unconscious biases to surface as you are responding based on what your beliefs are about that particular group.

Informal Instructional Data

Data from assessments aligned with curriculum and instruction is provided for teams through their curriculum. These assessments are built into the beginning, middle, and end of units. These are formal in nature, being that everyone takes them, and the criteria for success are the same for all students. Lesson plans also provide formal assessment opportunities in the form of quick and short written responses, multiple-choice questions, and more. We are seeking informal instructional data about the student experience. This requires going deeper than just asking students what they think about their learning. You have to ask questions aligned with not only the content and material but the execution and their connection to it. This is important because instruction is a multi-layered practice. You can have a highly rated curriculum, but there are many off-ramps for students that can impact their engagement with it. The way students feel about their teacher and their ability to access the material as well as their perceived usefulness of it in their daily life are two examples. Most importantly, the way a student believes a teacher sees their ability is paramount. The aforementioned are all catalysts that can impact assessment data, and this is why we need the informal data to tell us what instructional pivots are necessary that are not always obvious in the formal data. Surveying specifically for their needs will also help you to talk to teacher teams about possible needs and modifications where possible. We are looking to find out the culture and mindset around teaching and learning from the lens of those receiving the information. Can you change the curriculum if the kids feel like it isn't great? Of course not. You may not have a say in the curriculum at all. It is important, though, to use what you can from the data to improve its implementation. The sample survey below provides a starting point for questions you can ask *students* regarding curriculum and instruction:

TABLE 7.6 Student Curriculum and Instruction Survey

Materials and Resources

- Is your work presented (taught) in a variety of ways? (Video, articles, books, audiobooks, etc.)
- Do you have the ability to demonstrate (show) your learning in different ways? (Oral, written, video, etc.)

Connection to Material

- Is the material presented in a way that makes you feel like it will be valuable in real life?
- Are you being taught about people or concepts that are challenging and include varied problems and ethnicities?
- Does the material or concept make you think about larger world issues and possible solutions?

(Continued)

TABLE 7.6 (Continued)

Access and Entry Points

- Is the material provided in different ways so you can understand it?
- Are you provided with opportunities to work in groups or pairs?
- Do your peers support your learning through teaching, modeling, and explaining for you?
- If you are confused, does your teacher know? Do you think they have a plan of support for you?

Note: See Muhammad (2020) for her five pillars. Her model provides systems and structures for comprehensive planning on the teacher end. I would also suggest using the survey above to survey students about their experiences.

Informal School Culture Data

Talking to the young people in your building about what they are learning is important, but you also want to know how they are feeling in their spaces. This includes the classroom but also common spaces such as the gym, lunchroom, hallways, and so on. You really want to know how everyone feels about the culture of the building, and while there may be formal measures where staff can air their grievances or celebrate their community, these questions may be generalized and not specific to the information you desire to elicit. You really want to know if your community is a vibe! For example, asking "Do you trust your principal?" and providing a scale from 1 to 5, with 5 being yes and 1 being no, doesn't provide much information. A topic such as "trust" is one that should allow for open discourse and furthering the conversation. At minimum, an effective informal survey aligned with school culture should ask open-ended questions that result in more than a 'yes' or 'no'. Leadership and establishing/cultivating a culture are not objective processes. Neither, then, should the feedback be. What you ask depends on what you want to know as a leader. Have you noticed there are challenges with teachers working together in a specific department? Maybe the survey should focus on the leadership of that team or the lack thereof? Have you noticed parent engagement is lacking across the building? You should ask about the systems and structures for parent outreach and whether staff finds them effective. Creating an informal school survey should be driven by a challenge, something you desire to accomplish. It is important to determine what stakeholders would need to make it happen, as you should not enact policies or create change in a silo. Using your current noticings and desired outcome as the focus for your survey focus and questions allows you to use real-time data on the happenings of your community and examine them from the lens of wanting to improve challenges or affirm what is already working. An example of this would be the following:

TABLE 7.7 Survey Creation Formula

Current noticing + desired outcome = survey focus

TABLE 7.8 Survey Creation Formula Example

Current Noticing: Students are having trouble making it on time to their next class after the bell rings. +Desired Outcome: Wanting students to be in their classes on time	Survey Focus: Transitions for Students Question: We've noticed students are still in the hallway after the second bell. What can be changed to help them make it to their next class faster?

To the question above, teachers may state there are lots of students in the hallway at the same time and they commiserate instead of walking to class. Others may express needing more time in their periods to finish up lessons. If students were asked, they might say their program makes it so that their classes are not geographically close due to programming, thus taking them more time than the late bell allows because they have to cross multiple floors each period. In either scenario, using the noticing and desired outcome as the driving force allows you to demonstrate care and intentionality behind the questions being asked. More than seeking a general overview about "how are the hallways after each class," asking specifically with a problem/solution-oriented lens shows stakeholders you are not only observant but also responsive. You should also ensure that your surveys have multiple viewpoints for the same challenge. Asking teachers about the transitions and then asking students provide both perspectives and provide the space for crafting a response that addresses potential secondary or tertiary issues.

When creating your questions to use for informal data whether it be for parents, students, or staff, you as a culturally responsive school leader should always ask those who will take the survey what their noticings are and use this to drive the survey. We all know we don't have time to meet with every staff member and have a meeting about what should be on the survey and then a meeting to distribute the survey. Meetings are honestly the bane of my administrative existence. However, putting your ear to the streets to determine what is being "said" unofficially allows for a survey and measures that will include the voice of those who will ultimately be the arbitrators of the desired outcome. As an alternative to this survey, focus groups are also a fantastic lever for obtaining informal data on your community. You do not have to lead these focus groups—and I would argue that your presence would be a detriment to the data—but there should be someone designated to hold focus groups and ask questions about pertinent noticings. Focus groups also allow an element of freedom as things may come up in the ebb and flow of natural conversation that are not provided in a written survey. For example, if parents are being surveyed about their experience in the community, a focus group conversation would allow parents to extend their responses with additional questions posed by the interviewer. Whatever measure of informal data collection you use, it is important to center the experiences and viewpoints of various members of your community and lead with the desired outcome in mind. Focus on both things that can be improved but also reflect on and celebrate areas where things seem to be going well. Affirmation is a strong lever for building and maintaining a strong culture. The culturally responsive leader will practice distributive leadership while obtaining the information but will be the driving force of the overall process. Where possible, it is recommended that you be present at the onset to stress the importance of the survey as this will hopefully encourage most to complete it and be honest. The potential negative to this process relies on whether you are perceived as not acting on the data. Follow through on what you find and remember that if not you, then who? Appoint a designee and always follow up!

You have the formal and informal data, now what to do with it?!

After you spend the school year collecting data and doing nothing else, it is not enough to just look at the data and jump to action. The first step in the process for a culturally responsive leader requires you and your team to check your biases and be open and honest about when you are in your feelings and may be taking the data personally. You should also be aware of when there's a deference to explaining away the data versus talking through and accepting what it shows.

There should be a process where teams are allowed to unpack the data and reflect on what it says at face value (without any rationalization), what it implies (deeper examination), and whether everyone's voice was included. In order to have a true picture of the data and its implications, you want to make sure it is disaggregated (Fergus, 2017). Do you have varied races and ethnicities take the survey? Was everyone given a chance to be heard, whether they're from inside the school building or from outside"?

Did your leadership team take the survey? Did students of all identified subgroups (ENL/English language learner [ELL], special education, etc.) participate or have support with answering the questions? These questions are all important as leaving anyone out provides an incomplete picture and skews the data and perspective. This undermines your ultimate goal, which is determining how the building feels as a whole, not just for a particular subgroup of people. Disaggregation also allows you to posit the experiences of different groups against one another to take a better look at the differences. This may be telling in a way that is a wake-up call. Are your teachers of color having a harder experience with being included in collaboration than others? Are Latino students in special education scoring better than their peers of other racial groups? Unpacking the data in a way that is purposeful is just as important as collecting the information.

After you've evaluated, it is important to SHARE the data! What good are data and information about the community if you keep them to yourself? Sharing can be in the form of an overview with general feedback received and what it implies about the community. Sharing can also be in the form of sharing the results the way they came to you and explaining what you think they mean. Remember that parents and students aren't pedagogues, so the manner and language used should be inclusive and real to give the information solicited back to the streets. Technical terms allow for the perception that you are intelligent, but they do nothing for people who cannot decipher what you're trying to say. Don't muddle the message with jargon. Keep it honest, keep it simple, and don't make any immediate promises. Shifting a culture and making improvements for things such as curriculum and instructional moves take time. Start with one challenge at a time and let people know you value their voices and opinions. Culture takes a team and if you want it to be a VIBE, you have to do the day-to-day work one large endeavor at a time. The opposite of that is jumping to action and promising to address all the things that come from the survey. Once that doesn't happen because life be life'ing,[1] you will appear to be a leader who did not keep their word versus one who chose to take their time and be strategic. The choice is yours.

But How and When?

There's no hardcore timeline for examining data, especially data that is informal. Formal measures may require that you evaluate four times per year inclusive of baseline assessment and one end-of-year summative. As informal data is more comprehensive than numbers—at least if you're doing it correctly—my recommendation would be three times per year: once at the beginning of the year, one time at the midpoint, and again at the end. Unless new challenges arise, I would implore you to give the same survey so you can compare the results from each point. As there may be new challenges or changes, adding a question or holding a focus group to have a granular and focused view on said challenge may be the way to go. Are students absolutely losing their minds and you're seeing an increase in confrontations? Commiserate with the students for a focus group and see what's up as opposed to a whole-school thing. In this case, just focusing on students does not disparage the results so long as all student demographics are represented.

TABLE 7.9 Questions/Wonderings for Survey Creation

- What enduring issues are present in the community?
  - In common areas?
  - In classrooms?
  - At morning entry?
  - At dismissal?
- What are the experiences of various stakeholders in the community?
  - Parents
  - Students
  - Families
  - Teachers
  - Custodians
  - Office staff
  - Visitors
- What is the perception surrounding:
  - Curriculum
  - Relationships
  - Discipline
  - Collaboration
  - Leadership team(s)
  - Administration

"Data and Progress Monitoring: Numbers Don't Lie, Right?" Application and Materials

Progress Monitoring
Numbers Don't Lie, Right?

Entering	Emerging	Applying	Deepening
I use formal data measures to plan my goals for the school year. I evaluate these measures in isolation or with my cabinet/administrative team.	I use formal data measures for instructional shifts and other formal data (such as survey form state/jurisdiction) to plan for the school year. I evaluate these with a larger team, including teachers and team leaders.	I use formal data measures for instructional shifts as well as informal data measures such as surveys. I also use home-grown beginning and end-of-year surveys for staff. I evaluate these with a larger team and share the results with staff to inform change.	I utilize formal data measures, informal data measures, as well as staff informal surveys at varied points during the year, using input from stakeholders in creation. I disaggregate the survey data with a team and share the results without first jumping to action.

Activity

Applying the formula!
Use the formula below to create two informal questions you could ask based on your current community. Remember to think of a challenge you want to address.

Current Noticing:	Survey Focus:
+	=
Desired Outcome:	Question:

Scenario-Based Practice:

Data & Progress Monitoring

You have just reviewed the data, and after administering an anonymous perception survey about your leadership and that of your cabinet, survey shows that one of your administrators has low perception marks and staff feels like they can't trust her. What is your next step as a leader?

Think: *How will you go about unpacking this data with your cabinet? What is the next step in the evaluation of the data? How do you start the conversation?*

Books on Books on Books
What are you reading?

Note

1 Phrase meaning there are times when challenges are immeasurable and all things shift for the negative at once.

References

Feldman, J. (2019). *Grading for equity: What it is, why it matters, and how it can transform schools and classrooms.* Corwin, A Sage Company.

Fergus, E. (2017). *Solving disproportionality and achieving equity: A leader's guide to using data to change hearts and minds.* Corwin, A Sage Publishing Company.

Hammond, Z. (2015). *Culturally responsive teaching and the brain: Promoting authentic engagement and rigor among culturally and linguistically diverse students.* Corwin.

Ladson-Billings, G. (1995). Toward a Theory of Culturally Relevant Pedagogy. *American Educational Research Journal, 32*(3), 465–491. https://doi.org/10.3102/00028312032003465

Muhammad, G. (2020). *Cultivating Genius: An Equity Framework for Culturally and Historically Responsive Literacy.* Scholastic Teaching Resources.

8

Sustainability and Your Legacy

Were You Official?

The quiet truth about school leadership is that it requires one to have a special set of skills and receive nothing for them. Outside of intrinsic value, a forward career progression, and the desire to be in a position of authority, being a school leader is hard work every day. If you are locked in[1] and doing half of the things suggested in this book, you are exhausted consistently and in a constant quandary about what you should have or could be doing better every day. If you're a psychopath like my principal, you love every minute of the planning and decision-making. You thrive in the face of challenges and truly want to see people win—from the young people in front of you to the staff members who call you a leader. While being a leader is high-risk and low-reward, the joy comes in the face of knowing that every day you are making decisions that matter to students and families. You are creating a legacy that will last beyond your tenure, and even when you get it wrong, you can rest assured that you made the decision with the best of intentions at the time. It also doesn't hurt to know that, in many places, administrators/school leaders are paid well. Not nearly enough, but well.

The challenge lies in the fact that the educational landscape is constantly changing. Even from when I became an educator 10+ years ago, there has been so much change it feels as if I began teaching well before my years. As education continues to change and become even more tumultuous—looking at you Florida for saying "slaves developed skills that could be used for their personal benefit" (Najarro, 2023)—it is more important now than ever for school leaders who have culturally responsive lenses to take on these roles despite their apprehension. Those willing to develop their personal lens, be reflective, engage in uncomfortable conversations about race, and speak up in the face of injustices that impact their community both in the building and at large are needed in education more than ever. The reality, too, is all of this is exhaustive work and eventually it will be time to lay down the sword to let someone else take up the fight. Planning for your successor is never easy, but the work starts well before you are ready to go.

When you think of your successor, you should not be looking for someone who is just like you. You should be looking for someone who has the potential to be better. This doesn't mean you weren't an effective leader, it simply means you need someone who will have to address challenges you did not have to as they go further into their career. Remember those "changes" we spoke about? There are bound to be more that you cannot yet foresee. As you leave for your mimosas on the beach or that less stressful education consultant position (manifesting for myself here), your successor needs to be you on another level. Ideally, this person would be someone from within the community that you work closely with and have the opportunity to mentor and teach. Even if you are not able to be part of hiring your successor, having someone who is ready that you can vouch for allows them to be part of the conversation for the position. If that is not an option, you have at least replaced yourself in the field of education, and someone will be lucky to have them lead their community. This impact and mentoring reverberate, and the hope is that your mentee will go on to mentor others, thus creating a pipeline of strong leaders who are culturally responsive in their decisions and leadership. More so than the effectiveness of your mentee, reflecting on your community will tell you everything you need to know about your legacy and its impact. See Figure 6.1 in Chapter 6 regarding the process for selecting someone to mentor.

Did It Hit, Though?

So much of the job is driven by data and performance. The term "impact" is subjective as it can be measured through data that does not speak to your effect or relationships. If you're in a school that performs well on formal assessments, that can be used to speak to your legacy. Does that mean you as a leader developed your lens or leaned into uncomfortable conversations around advocacy for children of color or those with varied learning needs? Nope. What you should evaluate at the end of your tenure is whether the community is in a better place than when you found it. Shifts in culture and climate will undulate at a pace you can't predetermine. If you entered a community and were able to define clear core values that stakeholders aligned with and can speak to improvements aligned not just to instruction but also to culture, you have made great strides in that community. Other examples of a lasting legacy and positive impact are the perceptions of students and families aligned to their experiences and staff belief in your leadership. It takes a lot to build trust and be seen as an effective leader, especially when so much of your job involves managing more than actually controlling the outcomes. However, if you're like me and find it difficult to find positive things to say about yourself, below are some questions to ask yourself about your leadership and legacy:

Community Reflection

- → Did you make decisions based on your core values and the value system of the school community?
- → Did you have to compromise your integrity to achieve your ends?
- → Did culturally responsive education live in your building in various ways? (curriculum, relationships, etc.)
- → Did you engage stakeholders of all types? At all levels?
- → Did you center the needs of students of all demographics?
  - ◆ Race
  - ◆ Learning style
  - ◆ Economic status
- → Were you feared? Or respected?
- → If you saw a student or staff member in your day-to-day life outside of work, how would they respond to you?

The best measure of ensuring that your legacy is lasting is to engender a community that reflects your values and uses them in application for their daily interactions. Even if you have no involvement in who is hired, the community has already told you what it needs and you've hopefully supported and cultivated that by using a culturally responsive lens. Whoever is next will have to walk in their purpose and support the community in strengthening the foundation that has already been created. The best way to ensure that your legacy is lasting is to leave people behind at all levels who are about that life! Ensure that your community oozes the core values you weaved into its fabric, and no matter who succeeds you, they will have a challenge ahead. They'll have either a hell of a time trying to disrupt what you've built or a positive journey to make it even stronger. You should also determine if you impacted the surrounding community at large and not just the one in your building. Did you build relationships with the schools and businesses in your surrounding area? Did you include opportunities for politicians to support school initiatives and build pipelines for advancement of students and staff? Did you provide space for community vendors to facilitate workshops for parents and families? Do families plan, support, and lead events? These are all examples of leaving a legacy that extends beyond your role as school leader and shows that you subscribe to the ideals of "it takes a village" for an effective community approach to supporting young people.

The Ability to Pivot

Your legacy will also be contingent upon who you were as a leader when things got sticky. In times of challenge and turbulence, what was your approach? Did you pivot and consider the best possible outcomes for all parties involved, or did you default to what made you comfortable as a person, outcomes for the community be damned? Were you rigid and inflexible? "Ruling" with an iron fist and moving like a power-hungry dictator? The results will be wholly dependent on how you showed up but will be more so based on the decisions you made or did not make. One way to evaluate your legacy is to first know what type of leader you started as and where you landed. For example, I started as a leader full of "I know what's best" energy and had a very hard time understanding why adults weren't able to execute my flawless visions. I spent a copious number of hours crafting detailed documents and professional learning plans only to realize one thing: Yeah, I'm smart and the documents made sense to me, but did I truly provide access to teachers? My expectations were that adult learners would be able to pick up things quickly and move to implementation. Those who couldn't were the problem. The leader I am *now* understands that working with adults means I should take the same approach I took with my students. They should be seen for the attributes they bring and have those leveraged to support any initiatives. Their voices and expertise matter in all spaces, and they should be allowed to partner with others to build their own understandings. Probably most importantly, adults need love, too! While this will look different based on your leadership style, affirmation and celebration go a very long way. One question I always try to ask myself is would I want to work alongside me? While most would jump to answer "yes, of course," there were moments when my answer to that would have been "no." I was reclusive and standoffish and wanted to work only with students. I often saw things that rubbed me the wrong way and said nothing because it was easier than stirring the pot. Not the best position to take, by a long shot. As a leader now, I can say I am fortunate to be in a space where I can apologize when I'm wrong, take feedback, even when it puts me in my feelings because it still does sometimes, and be reflective. I've also learned to name my feelings and challenges where possible in order to have people understand me on a more personal level.

Making decisions has become a collaborative process unless my core values are being challenged. In those cases, we talk, we listen, we unpack, and we engage. I am transparent about my "why," and when it's best for kids but there's still apprehension, I try to focus my team on the intended outcome. All uncomfortable, but all money in the bank.

Legacy is EVERY DAY
I'm fairly new to this administrative life, so reflecting on my "legacy" might make some laugh. I'd argue, though, that your legacy is driven by how you are perceived in your community on a daily basis as well as when you are absent. As mentioned in Chapter 3 on the V.I.B.E, how you took inventory of the community needs, listened to or incorporated staff in the decision-making process, as well as leaned into your core values as part of your leadership will determine whether the school culture will continue to support systems and structures you intentionally set into place. Reflection on your legacy starts long before you even consider the possibility of taking on a new role or transitioning. *Daily*, you need to think of ways to reflect that challenge your viewpoints and make you think about the viewpoints of others. Your reflection also needs to be taken out of the isolation of just your thoughts. Sure, I talk to myself when I need expert advice, but it is important to include others in your reflection process as our Head, Heart, and Hands ultimately are measured by how we impact others. The constant reflection is imperative as it requires you to think of how your decisions and personhood at that time drove your thinking. Did you start leading your community at 25 and now are transitioning at 45? There is so much growth that happens for us as human beings that we cannot wait until the end of our tenure to determine whether we were fire! While there will be some discomfort associated with the constant self-check-ins, doing so at minimum *should* require us to ask questions of ourselves we may not otherwise have. Will we have the answers to these questions all the time? Absolutely not. The goal is to do the thinking aligned to your core values and the needs of those you've served and continue to serve daily.

Leadership and Legacy Reflection

→ What were the "blessings" you started with in your community?
- ◆ Did you leverage or cultivate these?
- ◆ Did you assess for "blessings" or just impart your vision?
  - What was the impact?

→ What does the data say?
- ◆ Formal testing data overall?
  - Disaggregated?
- ◆ Informal instructional data?
  - Disaggregated?
- ◆ Informal school culture data?
  - From students?
  - From staff?
  - From families?

→ Has there been a shift in culture?
- ◆ For the better?
- ◆ For the worse?

→ Are your leaders (administrative team, teacher team leads, etc.) able to sustain systems and structures in your absence?
- ◆ Do they take initiative to support others, or do they always defer to you for guidance?

→ Did you acknowledge and disrupt inequitable systems or give them a space to thrive?

While the reflection questions above are not exhaustive, they do provide a lens into your leadership and whether your presence is the deciding factor in the school's overall success. Being an effective leader means you are able to leave the building and what you've created sustains, thrives, and continues to grow with those whom you have worked alongside. A true measure of your legacy is if you can walk away from your position and objectively see your core values and those of the community represented. Overall, your legacy will be contingent upon your ability to look at yourself in the mirror as a leader and justify decisions you've made. From program implementation to hiring and staffing, even parent engagement initiatives. If your Head, Heart, and Mind are in the right place, there will always be things you wish you could have done differently. As I continue to work on my administrative legacy, I know there are still many areas where I can improve. I'd like to be viewed as a lead learner, willing to say the uncomfortable things necessary to achieve equity for children. Someone who will roll up their sleeves and get into the weeds—heels or high water! Overall, I want to leave a legacy as someone who cares for others and is intentional about showing love even when it needs to be tough. A safe space to land, but also a place where my colleagues know they can get this work if necessary all for the greater good. My teacher legacy? I get to see my core values represented in the students I continue to mentor and support through their young adult life.

What Grounds You?

As apathetic as I appear to be about leadership, I really do enjoy my job. I daily find ways to engage with students and lean into my core values of equity and realness. I am fortunate to be in conversations where my voice and viewpoints matter for children. I also know I've had moments where I needed to sit in the dark for a few hours just to decompress from a tough day. If you are someone who loves the game and sees yourself staying for a long time, it is important to reflect on what you do, or don't do, to ground yourself and refocus in times of turmoil. As a leader, you may not always have a listening ear that will not come back to haunt you. You may also have the opposite in a person who cares so deeply they run off all possible solutions when all you want is a moment to vent as a means of clearing your stream of consciousness. Whether you talk to a therapist, have a team of trusted colleagues who you have vent sessions with, or just do something as simple as journaling, you should always have an outlet for centering yourself and calming your "Head" so your "Heart" is in the right space. Operating from a space where you are continually stressed and burnt out can have adverse effects on how you show up. It can also impact your health. Outside of my family, my "center" is grounded in music. While my soundtrack will change depending on the time of year or my vibe, playing music always calms me and sets me up for success. I also have a morning routine when I walk into work that involves closing my office door and playing music for a bit before the day officially starts, but centering myself is something I had to learn the hard way. Remember, you are no good to anyone if you are burnt out, anxious, or irritable. Take stock of where you are as a person daily before you put your leadership hat on. I promise it's the best gift you can give yourself.

Legacy Building: Were You Official?

Entering	Emerging	Applying	Deepening
I work within my tenure and do what I can while I have the reigns.	I work alongside others and think of who else in the community has leadership traits.	I select a mentee based on their technical adaptability and skill set.	I intentionally select a mentee based on their core values and belief systems for children.
I trust that my community will be fine no matter who is in charge.	I reflect on school culture through the use of data.	I reflect on my legacy through the use of formal and informal data measures aligned to school culture.	I prepare them through exposure and real-world problem-solving in the community long before I intend to transition.
			I reflect on my legacy through sustainability with systems and structures.

The Work is Never done!
Reading that's Somethin' Light

Note

1 Hyper-focused on completing a task or goal.

References

Najarro, I. (2023, July 25). Florida's New African American History Standards: What's Behind the Backlash. *Education Week*. https://www.edweek.org/teaching-learning/floridas-new-african-american-history-standards-whats-behind-the-backlash/2023/07

Additional Reading

Love, B. L. (2023). *Punished for dreaming*. St. Martin's Press.

Marin, N. (2020). *Black imagination*. Mcsweeney's.

Sinek, S. (2014). *Leaders eat last: Why some teams pull together and others don't*. Portfolio Penguin.

Additional Resources

Additional Reads to Promote Equity and Shape Your Head, Heart, and Hands

Alex, P. (2022, July 5). Time to Pull the Plug on Traditional Grading? *Education Next*. https://www.educationnext.org/time-to-pull-plug-on-traditional-grading-supporters-say-mastery-based-grading-could-promote-equity/

Bryan-Gooden, J., Hester, M., & Peoples, L. (n.d.). *Culturally responsive English language arts curriculum scorecard*. https://steinhardt.nyu.edu/sites/default/files/2023-05/CRE%20ELA%20Curriculum%20Scorecard%202023.pdf

Costello, B., Wachtel, J., & Wachtel, T. (2019). *The restorative practices handbook: For teachers, disciplinarians and administrators*. International Institute for Restorative Practices.

Culturally Responsive Education Hub. (n.d.). Culturally Responsive Education Hub. https://crehub.org

Delpit, L. (2014). *Multiplication is for White People*. New Press.

Feldman, J. (n.d.). *A Call to Action for Equitable Grading SCHOOL GRADING POLICIES ARE FAILING CHILDREN*. Retrieved July 9, 2024, from https://crescendoedgroup.org/wp-content/uploads/2024/04/Call-to-Action-for-Equitable-Grading-Oct-2018-1.pdf

Hammond, Z. (2020). *Distinctions of equity*. https://crtandthebrain.com/wp-content/uploads/Hammond_Full-Distinctions-of-Equity-Chart.pdf

Heifetz, R. A., Grashow, A., & Linsky, M. (2009). *The practice of adaptive leadership: Tools and tactics for changing your organization and the world*. Harvard Business Press.

Khan, S. (2015). *Let's teach for mastery -- Not test scores*. Ted.com; TED Talks. https://www.ted.com/talks/sal_khan_let_s_teach_for_mastery_not_test_scores?utm_campaign=tedspread&utm_medium=referral&utm_source=tedcomshare

Minor, C. (2019). *We got this: Equity, access, and the quest to be who our students need us to be*. Heinemann.

Peoples, L., Islam, T., & Davis, T. (2021). *The culturally responsive-sustaining steam curriculum scorecard*. Metropolitan Center for Research on Equity and the Transformation of Schools. https://steinhardt.nyu.edu/sites/default/files/2021-02/CRSE-STEAMScorecard_FIN_optimized%20%281%29.pdf

Rubric for Culturally Conscious Decision-Making

Core Values and Self-Interrogation Who. Are. You?			
Entering	**Emerging**	**Applying**	**Deepening**
I understand the importance of feedback and receive it from my colleagues. I can acknowledge that my lived experience impacts my leadership and core values.	I understand the importance of feedback and receive/welcome it from everyone regardless of level and use it to reflect on my decisions and leadership. I can acknowledge that my race, ethnicity, and lived experiences impact my leadership and core values.	I seek/solicit critical feedback from the school community and reflect on how my perceptions or beliefs impact the decisions I make as a leader. I am intentional about exploring how my lived experiences may have created unconscious bias in my leadership/core values.	I seek/solicit feedback from all stakeholders and am also intentional about deepening my knowledge to disrupt negative narratives through literature, immersion, or "courageous conversations". I am aware of some of my unconscious biases, and I work to undo them and reflect on where these may show up in my leadership/core values.

Copyright material from Shauna McGee (2025), *Culturally Conscious Decision-Making for School Leaders: A Toolkit for Creating a More Equitable School Culture*, Routledge

Head, Heart, and Hands
Decision-Making

Entering	Emerging	Applying	Deepening
I understand the importance of making decisions for my community. As the leader, I make decisions objectively with the information I have available at the time.	I understand the importance of making decisive decisions for my community driven by school goals. I make decisions based on the moment and think about impact overall.	I make decisions and am transparent with my community about my rationale behind the decision being made. My core values are present in my decision-making, and I use my "head" and "heart" to inform my decisions.	Where possible, I seek/solicit input and feedback from stakeholders to inform my decision-making. My core values are present in my decision-making, and I also think through the impact on subgroups in my community.

What's the V.I.B.E?
School Culture Edition

Entering	Emerging	Applying	Deepening
I understand school needs based on information provided by higher-ups or those on my administrative team. I value and respect positional authority.	I assess a school based on tangible data points as they are objective. I value objective sources of data as subjectivity skews information.	I assess a school based on multiple data points, including data, observations, and stakeholder voice. In addition to objective data, I value the voices of those at different levels and understand that each person's opinion adds a different lens.	I assess a school based on the triangulation of objective and subjective data points inclusive of stakeholder voice. In response to data, I ask questions to challenge my own mental models and biases connected to my race and lived experience while unpacking noticings.

Copyright material from Shauna McGee (2025), *Culturally Conscious Decision-Making for School Leaders: A Toolkit for Creating a More Equitable School Culture*, Routledge

Rubric for Culturally Conscious Decision-Making ◆ 155

What ya Pockets Lookin' Like?
Budgeting

Entering	Emerging	Applying	Deepening
I make budgetary decisions based on enrollment numbers. I make decisions in isolation as I know what's best and have all the context.	I try to think of what I want the community should feel like when making budgetary decisions. I inform my administrative team of my decisions to obtain feedback after the fact.	I reflect on my core values in addition to the needs of my school community when making budgetary decisions. I make decisions in consultation with my administrative team/cabinet.	Through my core values and the needs of my community, I make decisions thinking of the least amount of adverse outcomes. I consult stakeholders and engage them in the decision-making where possible.

Is it a VIBE?
Curriculum and Instruction Edition

Entering	Emerging	Applying	Deepening
It's impossible to be an instructional leader as I oversee the school building and all its areas. Teachers are the arbitrators of knowledge, and I allow them to lead this conversation.	The region or district mandates my curricular choices, and I do not have a choice. I do not require modification or adaptation, as I see it as a deviation from the curriculum. I consult my administrative team about the curriculum and the process for implementation and feedback.	I evaluate all choices of curriculum presented alongside my department leads and administrative team. We then discuss what's best based on the community needs. I set my core values and school values at the forefront of the inquiry process.	I share my core values with stakeholders and name CRSE (culturally responsive-sustaining education) as a requirement. We together discuss the options available and determine what best meets the needs of the community. We have SHARED values that are represented in the curriculum/modification process.

Copyright material from Shauna McGee (2025), *Culturally Conscious Decision-Making for School Leaders: A Toolkit for Creating a More Equitable School Culture*, Routledge

Whose mans is this?
Capacity Building

Entering	Emerging	Applying	Deepening
The program is driven by student needs. Each team should report to me as the leader of the building for their inquiries and needs.	The program is created with teacher meeting time included. Each team should manage themselves as this is how people learn best and it builds interdependence. Team leaders serve as the "lead learners" and help lead others.	The program is created with students, teachers, and coaches in mind, centering collaboration and reflection time. Each team has an appointed "point person" to support and serve as an intermediary between administration. Team leaders are also continually supported through professional learning.	The program is a reflection of my core values as a leader and that of the school community. Team leaders are a reflection of stakeholders in different roles, not just administrative. Team leaders are provided with frequent inquiry cycles from teams to reflect on their vibe.

Progress Monitoring
Numbers Don't Lie, Right?

Entering	Emerging	Applying	Deepening
I use formal data measures to plan my goals for the school year. I evaluate these measures in isolation or with my cabinet/administrative team.	I use formal data measures for instructional shifts and other formal data (such as surveys form state/jurisdiction) to plan for the school year. I evaluate these with a larger team, including teachers and team leaders.	I use formal data measures for instructional shifts as well as informal data measures such as surveys; I also use home-grown beginning- and end-of-year surveys for staff. I evaluate these with a larger team and share the results with staff to inform change.	I utilize formal data measures, informal data measures, and staff informal surveys at varied points during the year using input from stakeholders in creation. I disaggregate the survey data with a team and share the results without first jumping to action.

Copyright material from Shauna McGee (2025), *Culturally Conscious Decision-Making for School Leaders: A Toolkit for Creating a More Equitable School Culture*, Routledge

Legacy Building:
Were You Official?

Entering	Emerging	Applying	Deepening
I work within my tenure and do what I can while I have the reigns. I trust that my community will be fine no matter who is in charge.	I work alongside others and think of who else in the community has leadership values. I reflect on school culture through the use of data.	I select a mentee based on their technical adaptability and skill set. I reflect on my legacy through the use of formal and informal data measures aligned with school culture.	I intentionally select a mentee based on their core values and belief systems for children. I prepare them through exposure and real-world problem-solving in the community long before I intend to transition. I reflect on my legacy through sustainability with systems and structures.

For Product Safety Concerns and Information please contact our EU
representative GPSR@taylorandfrancis.com
Taylor & Francis Verlag GmbH, Kaufingerstraße 24, 80331 München, Germany

www.ingramcontent.com/pod-product-compliance
Lightning Source LLC
Chambersburg PA
CBHW052341230426
43664CB00041B/2602